Water Workout

For Caz, water honey

Water Workout

120 Water Exercises for Swimmers and Nonswimmers

BILL REED WITH MURRAY ROSE

Harmony Books
New York

The publishers wish to thank the City of Prahran, and in particular the kind cooperation of Jim Harley, for use of its swimming pool for the photographs.

Published in the United States in 1986 by Harmony Books, a division of Crown Publishers, Inc., 225 Park Avenue South, New York, New York 10003.

Originally published in Australia by Sun Books, The Macmillan Company of Australia Pty. Ltd., 107 Moray Street, South Melbourne 3205.

HARMONY and colophon are trademarks of Crown Publishers, Inc.

Library of Congress Cataloging-in-Publication Data

Reed, Bill, 1942 –
   Water Workout.
   Includes index.
   1. Aquatic exercises. I. Rose, Murray. II. Title.
GV505.R385 1985   613.7'1   85-30498

   ISBN: 0-517-56183-2

First American Edition

Photographs by Henry Jolles
Design by Sue Bates

Contents

Foreword by Murray Rose   7

Introduction   9

1. Why Water?   13

2. Water Exercising, That's Why   16

3. How to Use This Book   20

4. Feeling Yourself Feeling Good   22

5. Water Exercising, Music, Aerobics?   28

6. Water Exercising and Swimming   29

7. Water Exercising and the Cold   30

8. Helpful Devices for the Super-fit and Not-so-fit   31

9. The Exercises: Easy-to-Intermediate Levels   33

10. The Exercises: Intermediate-to-Advanced Levels   62

11. Your Water Body: Beauty and Body Development   80
   Arms and Shoulders: upper arms, 81; lower arms, 83; shoulders, 85; wrists and hands, 87
   Back: spine, 88; back muscles, 89; buttocks, 91
   Legs: calves, 93; feet and ankles, 94; groin, 96; hips, 97; hamstring, 98; knees, 100; thighs (front, rear, inner), 101
   Stomach and Chest: abdomen, 104; chest (lungs), 106; side muscles (laterals), 107; waist, 109
   Neck: 110

12. For Couples   111

13. Pregnancy   123

14. For Arthritis, Injuries, Joint Disorders   136

15. The Natural Environments   145

Index to Exercises   147

Index   150

Foreword

Water is my friend, my mistress, my shrink, my physician and my priest. It is my passion and my addiction. Life without a daily splash is unimaginable. The morning does not officially begin for me until I climb into the shower. If I end the day without a dip, all is not right with my world.

I am sure that I'm not alone in my love affair with water. Swimming is always near the top of the list of our favourite recreational activities. There is a universal fascination with water and water sports. It runs deep in our soul — and our body. After all, we're mostly made up of the wet stuff.

The only surprise is that there are many people who have still not discovered the real joys and benefits of water. There are two possible reasons: fear and fear. Non-swimmers are afraid to let themselves go and fully explore the feeling of water. It remains a foreign element. Serious swimmers (most lap swimmers are serious) are also afraid to experience the deep sensual pleasure of water because they are too busy getting the job done.

At the grand old age of eighteen months I traded in my bathtub for Sydney Harbour. I never did get too much of a kick out of rubber duckies, but the sun and the sand and the sea were an invitation to an endless variety of games. So began an adventure that eventually led me to play in oceans and lakes and rivers and hundreds of pools and ol' swimmin' holes around the world. It was all pure fun — that is, until I made the mistake of winning one too many gold medals. After that, the game became work. There was suddenly a lot at stake. My parents, my coach, my friends, my country and, most of all, myself were counting on me to win. No more fooling around; this was the big time. I was on the road to becoming another worn-out, disillusioned jock, looking forward to the day when I could hang it up for good. Fortunately, fate took a turn. I was beaten in a high-stakes race in the Rome Olympics. For a moment my world caved in. I wanted to toss in the towel. When the spray settled I realized that I could never give up swimming, but I could give up the obsession of winning at any cost. I found that my love for water was stronger than my love for competition. A strange thing happened. I swam faster than I ever had in my life, and it was fun again.

This book may or may not make you a better swimmer. It may or may not give you a body beautiful. What it will do is to open up the world of water play for you and help you feel just plain good about yourself. Whether you're a non-swimmer or a potential Olympic champion, it's about time you had an intimate relationship with water. It might even save your life, and it's bound to put a grin on your face.

Water is a wonderful tranquillizer. We all know how restful it is to watch the movements of the ocean or listen to the babbling of a brook. We know the relaxation from taking a hot bath. The next step is to actively use the healing qualities of water to increase our well-being. I defy anyone to hold onto their worries while exercising in water. Try it.

You will find it next to impossible. The water entices you into a state of surrender that melts away tensions. Call it therapy, if you like, but we need all the help we can get to keep our sanity intact. Learning how to flow with the water is a great teacher of how to flow with life. The gentle resistance of water not only trains our muscles, but also our emotions and our minds to cope with the everyday grind.

The number one problem facing modern man (and woman) is stress. It's a killer. We will do or pop or drink or submit to almost anything to escape from our tensions. Anyone who claims to have an answer is made an instant guru. Just keeping up with the latest fads is enough to give you an ulcer. Among the most respectable, and most enduring, activists of the anti-stress movement are the 'fitness freaks'. Far be it for me to denigrate fitness. I have often been accused of having an unnatural alliance with the deity of health. I draw the line, though, at joining in the current battle of 'no pain, no gain'. The excessive pumping and jogging and straining of our bodies can do more damage than good. If the cost of fitness is increased stress, it defeats the whole purpose of an exercise program.

The key to total fitness is 'effortless effort'. You don't have to be a Zen master to feel the inner rhythm of your body in the water. You will be guided by the water to tap into your intuitive knowledge of how to coordinate your movements with less effort. As you learn to tune yourself with water you will discover how easy it is to direct your energy. Then any work you do will have a far greater payoff in terms of physical fitness and psychological ease. Yes, fitness does require exertion, but unless it is correctly applied most of our effort is wasted. If I'm going to work myself up into a sweat I want it to count for something. Struggling and fighting don't make it against the passive resistance of the water. You know that, if you have ever been caught in a riptide. The only effort that really counts in water, or anywhere else for that matter, is every part of the body working together as a unit.

In the semi-weightlessness of water many of the restrictions we experience on land are removed. You will be amazed at what you can do when you make friends with water. Just let the kid in you out to play. Water will do the rest. You will find yourself recapturing the natural skills you were born knowing. Greater vitality, greater confidence, even greater self-awareness are available to you from the right and regular use of your water gym.

Last one in's a mug!

Murray Rose

Introduction

At the time that this book was published, there hasn't been all that many publications which have specialised in water exercising for both swimmers *and* non swimmers.

That has been very surprising. Water has not been just the element that human beings have gone back to through some supposed evolutionary instinct. Nor has it just been the element that human beings have gone back to on a hot day, in order to sit placidly in it with a cool drink in one hand and a book in the other. When you think about it, water has been the element that human beings have gone back to in order to enjoy themselves vigorously – to jump around in, to splash and romp, to play around like children. We've all seen it; we've all done it.

Many of us have pools in our very own homes – or, if not, there are the public swimming pools or the beaches or the lakes and rivers we use. By simply enjoying ourselves in them, we are exercising in them to a great and unrealised benefit. Just treading water requires a degree of effort and stamina that you'd be surprised about. You've sensed it does, especially if you're not a great hand at swimming, yet you've probably previously thought, 'Oh well, the pool's for the kids or those guys thundering up and down those lanes'.

Not anymore. The water exercise realisation is growing throughout the world. And it's about time. Many things make water the ideal fitness medium – and, if you've absorbed the routines in this book and got enough of them tucked away under your belt, so to speak, then you'll soon learn why water exercises are about the best all-round exercising you could ever do.

And if you've already got a pool, you've already got an ideal fitness medium!

The Gym You Already Have

In home pools alone, there are just as many 'gyms' around the country as there are home dryland gyms. I have called these pools gyms, and I hope you're going to be pleasantly surprised at the great variety of uses you can put it to and so help the fitness and well-being of yourself and your family. There's nothing magical in the concepts of pool gyms and water exercising, either.

It is really only a matter of looking at your pool as having another use than a place just for your children's or your suntan's or your neighbors' use. Think of your pool gym as the gym you've already paid for. When there's no children splashing around in the pool and when the partying around it is over, it can be used in its 'downtime'.

Furthermore, your pool gym can give you fitness without the sweaty pain and strain of land-locked gyms because that's what water *does*. It's where your limbs and muscles and joints can relax and be soothed for once, before beginning to recover that suppleness that you thought time had robbed you of once and for all.

That pool gym that you've got sitting somewhere out the back is probably the best gym you could ever want to buy for love or money, anyway.

Quite apart from water being arguably the best element for exercising in for any of us – young, old, super-fit or ill – your water gym doesn't demand joining fees or going public in the latest expensive outfits, or getting involved in an all-in, all-eyes club atmosphere. If you're away from offendable eyes, you can even water exercise in the nude if it's your own pool gym. You can water exercise together (see Chapter 12). You can do it to music. You can do it gently and soothingly or you can do it for body building.

Buy an inexpensive lightweight wetsuit and you can even do it all winter. And, if you get more than slightly embarrassed by the public show of running or jogging in public, why don't you try running up and down or on the spot in your own private no-sweat-but-rigorous, convenient pool? There's no divine necessity to throw your body around public places at all.

So, one of the major messages of this book is to get you to think of your pool as something that can also work for you, not just play for you.

It's a Gym

Many of us don't have home pools, of course. We use public swimming pools or private club pools. Well, that's okay, too.

Exercise in them. You don't have to just float or swim around in them. If you're a swimmer, swim *and* also water exercise. Float *and* also water exercise. Even train *and* water exercise.

If you think about it, it's curious how many of us already mostly use those public facilities for exercising in anyway. We don't even know we are. The next time you're down there, just take a look around. Only a small minority is actually swimming; a few others are floating or standing around cooling off. But most are in there whoopeeing it up with a display of carefreeness that we wouldn't be seen dead doing in, say, a public park. Those people are enjoying themselves, sure, but what they're really doing is exercising in a nice, chaotic way. They're responding to the water and burning up energy. It mightn't be exercising to any set routine that any of us know, but it's exercising (that is, moving their bodies around in energy-ridding ways) nonetheless.

That's why water exercising in pool gyms is only building on the what-comes-naturally, anyway.

Also, being able to swim laps has nothing to do with it. Swimming and water exercising are not the same thing. You can do the great majority of the exercises in this book even if you can't swim; and with a little commonsense you can do almost all of them.

Water exercising, if you're only a reasonable swimmer or not a swimmer at all, allows you to come into your own in your own or your local pool.

You won't be alone. Your public pool will already be being used extensively for synchronised swimming exercises and routines, for additional nonswimming exercises to aid swim training, and for your local beefy sports team as a variety to their daily training schedules. You mightn't see them; they're probably done in a different time of the day. But they do water exercising, and they're there being just as sensible as you.

Even down at your local fitness gym or country club, think about that pool facility you've got there and which takes up a considerable amount of those expensive subscriptions each year. Instead of using it as somewhere you cool off in or taper off after your massage, use it properly. *Exercise* in it. You're paying for using supplied fitness media, so use the pool gym too.

Modern Water Exercising

Water exercising has graduated from the image of the hospital physiotherapist's pool. Competitive swimmers, water polo players, synchronised swimmers, people with injuries . . . these are nowhere near the only ones doing water exercises these days. Non-swimmers are using exercise classes down at the local pool to get as much fitness, strength and toning as swimmers. Contact sports people like footballers, boxers etc are taking some part of their training in the pools. Pregnant women are taking to water with great relief and pleasure for reasons that are obvious to anyone who watches them move with sudden, relieved freedom.

The elderly are banding together to experience the pleasure of once again being able to exercise in ways they thought were long behind them.

The wiser of the competitive swim coaches are bringing water exercises more and more into regular training sessions.

Even on the more recreational/fitness/razzamatazz side, there is the mushrooming of water disco music sessions; they're good and fun and therapeutic and come under various trade-mark names. They're for all ages and sizes and physical standards and physiques – and they're great to watch.

Some months ago, I did watch one of these music-led water exercise classes. The music was as hot a disco sound as you would ever hear downtown on a Saturday night. The people in the class were hardly a potential substitute cast for the latest Breakdance movie, I can assure you, yet they looked really good jumping, hopping, gyrating around with punchy arms and legs going this way and that.

They did a whole nonstop 40-minute session, and they were still smiling with delight at themselves and each other when they'd finished. They were tired but they weren't exhausted; no way.

It was me who got the shock when they came out of the pool. It had actually been a class for physical rehabilitation. Some of them were really old; some really over-fat; some really physically disabled; and some really looked like they'd just gone through a major illness.

But they'd just had the joy of water, and the joy of water exercising. And I couldn't help but wonder what they would have looked like if they'd tried to do the same 40-minute routine in a dryland gym.

There are many pool gyms around you. You only have to come to realise the fun and great benefit of exercising in water to seek one out.

You'll be amazed how many others are already using that pool for its ultimate benefit – your own wellbeing and the wellbeing of your loved ones.

11

1

Why Water?

Water won't give you the ultimate in body-building muscles. If you're into the bulging-muscles look, whether you're male or female, a dryland gym is best for you – for that sort of action which will take you years. Water won't give you those special sports looks – like the legs of a distance runner or the forearms of a tennis player or the thighs of a footballer.

What water *will* give you so readily is great overall muscle toning and conditioning for much less time, effort and specialisation. You'll call that shapeliness if you're a woman, and all-round ruggedness if you're a male. This is because water gets more muscles *going* for any one exercise than any other medium.

More specifically, there are far more general body exercises able to be done by you in water than elsewhere, in which most, if not all, of the muscle groups are given healthy flexing. Most of these general body exercises are the floating/swimming ones, to be sure. However, you just think about the simple water routine of holding on to the side of your pool at arm's length and doing, say, five minutes of kicking; where else can you exercise your legs to such vigorous degree, from feet right up to the hips? You are also giving great stretch or flex to your stomach, your side muscles, your back, your neck, and your shoulders.

That's because water has buoyancy. Even if you keep your feet on the bottom, water has buoyancy for you. We think of buoyancy in swimming terms, but what it really does is to allow you to do things in water that you can not do on land. It frees you from the tugging of gravity. You know that and I know that, but your muscles and your joints don't 'know' that like they sure as heck 'know' how heavy gravity is. Let's take, say, your hip. It doesn't 'know' that you're doing leg-up exercises on your workout room floor or in your pool gym; it doesn't 'know' that when it is suddenly swung through a much greater arc and with much less strain, it's because of the water in the pool gym. In suppleness, in fitness benefit, the same hip can appreciate it, though.

Water, the Great Communicator

Exercise is movement with some strain. Good exercise is good movement, good strain. Water allows you greater movement with less strain.

It's not only buoyancy that makes your pool a great gym. Water not only takes the strain, but imparts a flexible resistance to you. If you move faster in water, you will meet greater resistance to your movement. If you want to take it gently, you will feel that special 'soft' resistance that we all recognise as soothing, relaxing.

This means that if you want to do your routines slowly and lovingly (you might feel like that, even if you're superbly fit but have had too good a time the previous night), then water will respond to you that way. It gives your mood back to you. On the other hand, if you want to use your pool gym for hard, rugged, aggressive exercises, water will give that back to you too – in the form of muscle strength, endurance and power.

Because water responds to you by way of its automatic or non-mechanical resistance, it *communicates* with you. It echoes your feelings, your intentions. So if you want all-round beauty or good strong looks, it will help you get them. If you want a bigger bust or a bigger chest, that's okay too. Set the basic goal through the exercises you choose and you can adjust the resistance you want by sheer feel. You don't need all those expensive isometric and isotonic apparatus that are all the thing these days, yet unfortunately come costly either to buy or through those expensive club fees.

Water itself is the only 'apparatus' most people ever need.

So Easy On You

Try to remember that water is friendly and you will find it very enjoyable to go about your water exercises. As much as water lets you dictate the resistance you want out of it, so it lets you exercise without the same sore after-effects of dry land. Remember the times when you've had a dryland burst of unusual activity of, say, playing ball in a park or having to row a boat hard, and so forth? The next day you really feel it. You're as stiff as all heck, and don't you ever know and show it.

At the same time, remember back to the many, many times you've hopped into a pool or the sea and cold-turkeyed jumping, crashing, fooling around in mad bursts that, when you think about it, add up to a much more strenuous exercising than those ball-in-the-park, rowing-a-boat situations. You're very rarely stiff the next day; in fact you often feel great.

That's water. It's your soother, the 'bath' of your body and mind, the water grail, not grave. It is not for nothing that the enveloping powers of water are used as universal psychotherapeutic tools.

So Stern on You, Too

Make no mistake, though, water is no weak or effeminate medium, as it's often been thought to be.

There is one simple experiment you can do to prove that to yourself: Hold your arms outstretched and together in front of you and pull them back to their open-arm limit. Repeat this a few times as vigorously as you can. Then do the same thing standing in shoulder-depth water, cupping the palm of your hands 'against' the water with each forward and backward pull or push. Do this a few times as vigorously as you can. You'll feel how you're *heaving* against the water.

The more beefy you are, the more beefily you have to heave.

It's no weak medium, that's for sure. You can make water as stern on you as you want to be stern on yourself and do it under a condition of natural self-regulation.

Exercising Benefits

When you're exercising, you are trying to do any number of things. Essentially, however, good exercising benefits you for *endurance* (ie, you can last longer); *strength* (ie, you can be stronger while lasting longer); *resilience* (you don't have to wait so long before you get up and at 'em again); *energy loss* (while you're going longer and stronger and sooner, you're slimmer).

If you're that huge beefy hunk of a footballer, and you can do the simple fanning of the arms exercise I've mentioned earlier for ten minutes with all the *heave* you've got in you, you'll sure get a feeling of the endurance, strength, resilience and energy loss to come.

But if you're a svelte snippet of a thing and want to stay that way, thank you, then you can do the same exercise nice and gently and get more endurance, strength, resilience and energy loss out of it than you would doing it on dry land.

You can get all the special needs you want for yourself at your fingertips in your pool gym. See the section on 'Your Water Body' for this. However, water is not just for you alone. There's your family or your loved ones and they might have special needs, too.

Special Needs

In the past it's been thought that water exercise is only for therapy; that it's that sickly medium that healthy people shouldn't be seen dead in, not even in a hospital.

The greatest thing about the modern awareness of using pools for good, strong general fitness is that it's shown us that the elderly, the disabled, the recuperating, the immobilised and the uncoordinated have known something more than us. They've known the great things about exercising in water for generations.

The nicest thing about being shown up in that way is that we, in our turn, are now showing those fitness experts (I include many swim coaches in there, too!) and those carefree, pool-hogging frolicking kids of ours that we can do it too – and do it just as well and enjoyably.

Even so, there are people who can *only* exercise in the wonderful thing that water is – and there are far more than generally realised. In your family or in your circle of friends there are always likely to be those who have had an accident and who can get immeasurable benefit from doing the right and *unhurting* routines in the pool. There are Mum and Dad who would love to exercise to be as young as they feel, but are embarrassed to do so out of the covering that water gives, and the general protection against exercise injury that water gives. There is that beautiful pregnancy that must be taken care of through proper exercising, yet the thought of bouncing baby-to-be around on dry land is repulsive . . . so there's the *caring* that water gives. There are even the super-fit who just need a break without lowering the rigor of their training.

Water transmits its own attention. All anyone needs is a general idea of what is wanted out of it. This is why water communicates.

Hopefully this book will give you the building blocks of that communication.

Work out your exercises, and enjoy. Improvise your exercises, and still enjoy. Work out your own routine and the right vigor and repetitions you want to do, and enjoy. Above all, return the communication of water by listening to it. Yes, *listening to it.*

I am not speaking psychically when I say that. If you learn to listen to the water 'beats' that you make, you will switch on to the natural rhythm that your individual exercising has. It will give you your own cadence and your own yardstick of what you should be doing today over yesterday. You will then be returning the communication.

But don't make any unnecessary splashes. I once had a swim coach who told me, 'You swim alright, but you disturb the water so much!'. In water terms, that's impolite!

2
Water Exercising, That's Why

What you won't find in this book are day-by-day, week-by-week, month-by-month fitness programs that you should either follow religiously or go out back and commit hara-kiri.

These so-called 'programs' or 'schedules' that you get thrown at you are usually worked out along the lines of the perfect, average type. They say that you should be doing so-and-so exercise so many times on day one, or week two, etcetera, in combination with these-or-those other exercises. By day three or week two you should be doing the same exercise this number of times and should be looking to combine it with these other exercises given in this chart or this list. Not only that, you should be able to be doing these at such-and-such rate with this heartbeat during that rest period or other. All you have to do is keep consulting the many charts. And all you should be is the perfect, computerised, average shape, size, age, outlook, capability, lifestyle etcetera, etcetera.

At the end of it, you should have lost so many pounds or kilograms (it doesn't matter where you live!) and your biceps should look like the front cover photograph or your hips should be good swanking sights along Hollywood Boulevard; and you should have changed your whole outlook, not to mention your eating habits (and, oh yes, all those social comforts and contacts you've built up over a whole lifetime!), to keep faith with the New You. And, if you haven't, then it's not the book's fault, you're told. It's yours. You don't measure up to what the book says you ought to be.

The model, the Average, has taken over the fitness business.

The circuit-training syndrome has taken over from commonsense.

For example, you might not *want* to do this-or-that exercise today. You mightn't feel like it. You might be feeling so ropey or tired or angry or lethargic that to do this-or-that exercise three more times than you did yesterday is just a huge, regimented bore. Then again, you might be incapable of getting any sort of normal human coordination before breakfast or before your fourth cup of coffee (with real sugar!), let alone spring out of bed pretending to be happy or alive and alert and muesli-bound. You might like to down a few beers or sip a brandy, lime and soda after work every day, without feeling guilty that you're not out on your particular dryland gym and sweating it out over yesterday's inhuman efforts.

If you do, that's good. That's cool. That's you. And no regimentation of routines and schedules and programs is going to chart what will make you healthier.

Be Your Own Coach

A general fact of existence is that you are the best judge of yourself. You know when you are exercising really well. You can feel when it is doing you good. You can even feel when you're slacking. Nobody can tell you what is the right path of fitness for you. Except you, and you do that absolutely naturally.

When you're feeling low, but you still get up and get into exercising, nobody but you can know how much of an effort – let's call it mental fitness – you've overcome to do that.

Nobody can understand the special feeling of achievement – let's call it fitness wellbeing – that you experience having done it. It doesn't matter whether you beat yesterday's performance or lived up to the chart on page 157 of some book or other. The point is you've beaten today. You've beaten yourself.

And if that's not fitness, what is?

What You will Find in This Book

We make no attempt to give the number of repetitions you should do, nor the time you should do them in, nor the rest periods you should keep to.

We make no attempt to put exercises into programed 'sets', either.

Most dryland programs, to be fair, have to give some sort of progression of doing the exercises so that you don't do yourself damage by exerting strain on some muscle before you've stretched it or warmed it up. That's quite right, too, because of the gravity – the *jolting* – factor on dry land.

Water though has that buoyancy, that minimised gravitational factor. Providing you start out sensibly on the stretching exercises, then do a bit of warm-up – if you haven't done it already – before you move on to the more strenuous or flexing routines, you'll be pretty alright in water. It's soft. For any one exercise, however simple, it also generally exercises more muscles and joints than those dryland efforts. And what other muscles benefit generally relies on your individual 'water-style'. That's the other beauty of water exercising – its individuality.

In this book, we have merely lumped some of the thousands of possible exercises you can do in your pool gym according to whether we feel they are easy or require a good deal more of what it takes. For obvious reasons, we have also indicated those that only swimmers can do and those that non-swimmers can do. We've done those two things in these ways: There are chapters on Easy-to-Intermediate exercises and on Intermediate-to-Advanced exercises. For swimmers, each exercise has a notation: 'Floating'. For non-swimmers, there's the notations of 'Standing' or 'Standing/Holding on to the side' or 'Floating/Holding'.

You should choose your own sets of exercises. You might want to vary them day-by-day because that's the type of person you are. You might like to do the same set of exercises every day, but bettering yourself each time in either vigor or repetition or duration, because that's the type of person you are. You might like to do one or two on every second page because that's the way you like it, and so on.

It's up to you. You know yourself. You know when you are starting to feel really good, or feel so down that, even doing one or two, you're doing yourself pretty proud which, to my mind, is getting fit. That's being the best coach you have – yourself.

The Only Suggestion: Regularity

The only suggestion we'd make is to try to give yourself a set water workout pattern from day-to-day or whatever time suits you. Any benefits to be got from any exercise program will be hit-and-miss if you don't keep it up.

Try to establish a water-exercising pattern to your life. It could be a set time in the water every day, or another set time every other day. It could be morning, lunchtime, after work. Like anything that is giving you great benefit, though, you ought to protect its place in your life by giving it priority over all but the most essential other activities. You'll soon start to feel that something is amiss if you're not exercising, but initially you really do need to be disciplined about it.

If you set yourself a particular time and place, then you'll reap regular benefits from a regular routine and regular program. It's up to you. If you concentrate on variety when exercising, you'll easily be able to keep up your interest and challenge, whether you're in the water for meditation, play or a hard workout.

Generally, it's thought that about 40 minutes at what they call the 'working heart rate' gives top benefit. But you'll know when you've had enough and when you're overtaxing that old ticker, anyway. You do that instinctively. Just, perhaps, gradually build on that time and the compression of exercises you fit into it.

That goes for the strongest and fittest of any of you, too. Know yourself. You're big enough – and probably wise enough – to control your own exercise content and regimen.

By vigor or otherwise, just let water know what you want out of it and it will respond. Apply vigor to water and you'll get it back instantaneously.

That applies even if you are in an aquatic class down at your local pool or fitness club. Your instructor or coach can only show you the way and the doing of the exercise. He or she won't be able to indicate to you the real vigor you should put into each exercise. The communication between you and water is too personal for that.

You are in a one-to-one relationship with the water in your pool gym. Use it as you want it to be used for the result that you want out of it . . . for yourself or your loved ones.

Developing The Parts You Specially Want To

Talking about results, we have added sections to this book which show you how to develop those parts of your body you wish further developed. You will find these in Chapter 11.

If you want to develop your thighs or tighten your buttocks, or whatever, you can look up the appropriate anatomical heading and get the range of exercises we recommend for those purposes.

Make no mistake about it: water is superb for beauty and body toning for the male or female 'attractive look'.

Breathing

Water exercising helps you to breathe more deeply, and breathing deeply and regularly is a great regulator of feelings of wellbeing and being able to cope in your everyday life. 'Take deep breaths and count to ten' is more of a truism than just a Grandmother's saying. We would not find so many situations at home or the office so stressful if we stepped back for a moment and controlled with deep breathing that rapidly increasing metabolic rate of our body. We could minimise those 'rushes of blood to the head', control better the pumping of adrenalin and noradrenalin that produces those unwanted 'highs'. Likewise, any exercising that imbues our everyday selves with deeper and more regular breathing is a great benefit. Water exercising can be the best.

The fact is that most adults have forgotten how to breathe properly. You only have to watch a child while he or she is sleeping. They breathe from the bellies and seem to float on air.

When doing your water exercises, try to do the same. Pay attention to your breathing at all times, even if you are exercising in the shallow end of the pool. Gulp in the air at any time your abdomen muscles contract — that is, in the action phase of the exercise. Really blow out the air when your abdomen muscles relax in the relaxation phase of the exercise. If you are blowing out under water, really explode those bubbles out through your mouth and nose; use the evidence of the bubbles as an indicator of how well you are breathing out. You can really get up a good and invigorating rhythm of gulping air in and forcing it out.

So remember this underlining factor to all your routines: Get a breathing pattern. Exhale on action phase. Inhale on relaxation phase.

Keeping and Restoring Health and Beauty

Water exercising is one of the very few popular activities that not only strengthens the external muscles, but also the internal muscles and organs. Such a combination of internal and external exercise energises the whole body, and helps restore or keep health and beauty.

We lose energy during the day just through our daily habits — and this is what living is all about. However, one form of energy loss that is not beneficial is actually through *incorrect* exercise. Exercise is incorrect if it creates any type of physical imbalance that short circuits the flow of creative and/or natural energy loss. This imbalance is the root of disease. Of course, there are many philosophies with practical applications designed to restore that balanced energy flow, and physical exercising in general is one of them . . . but water exercising is one of the few specific activities open to all of us. As an old Chinese proverb says: 'If you do external exercise, you must do internal exercise. If you do internal exercise, you may do external exercise'.

Diet and Weight Loss

Many experts will also try to tell you that water exercising is not all that efficient when it comes to the slimming aspect of fitness, or the take-off-the-flab routines. This is a great misconception that should be laid to rest once and for all. Weight comes off you simply because of the amount of energy you use over and above the amount of energy you take in through eating. At any same ratio of energy output and time taken, you will lose as much weight exercising in water as on dry land. In fact, in my opinion you will lose more because you will be able to keep going all that time with much fewer breaks. And don't fall for the statements that you can give more to an exercise on dry land than in water. Get aggressive with water when you're doing any one exercise and see if you can get away with a gentle expenditure of energy!

Water exercising is also a great assistance to losing weight, because it complements diets so well. It is an ideal activity to maintain muscle toning while dieting. Done properly and regularly, it tends to decrease the appetite. It is generally thought that this is because you're feeling much better in yourself; you're losing weight; your blood is being cleared of excess fats and unwanted waste products because you're not stressed nearly so easily; your blood pressure is going down and you've got more energy during the day. You're still feeling hungry, but it's a healthy hunger. You feel it's positively against what you want and need to eat unhealthily, or to keep up the pattern of some unhealthful addiction.

Water Works!

Unlike animals, human thirst is not always a reliable signal for the water our bodies need. This is because our thirst does not keep up with our water loss. Yet we should be drinking more. Even when we're not thirsty — and particularly when we are dieting — we should drink more water to keep our systems flushed. What's more, water has no calories, so even the occasional mouthful of pool water you might get from water exercising won't do you or your dieting any harm! It's the increased thirst factor that will be doing you added good.

Those Special Needs Again

This book would only be attempting to try the impossible if it endeavored to give all the beneficial exercises available to anyone of any age and any physical condition. Having said that, we do not apologise for giving different chapters for special-needs people, like the pregnant woman, the recuperating accident victim, the unfortunate arthritis sufferer. Why should we? We've got the perfect gym for them. Their nearest pool.

It goes without saying that special-needs people should pop along to their doctor to get both a physical checkup and a bit of doctorly advice before attempting any exercise. We all should do this, whether we are starting out or by way of regular checkups.

Having said that, our advice to everyone, including the special-needs people, is to feel the water, communicate with the water, enjoy the water, and come to understand your own needs in your own way and with your own timing. In water, do what you want to do in the best and most honest and enjoyable way. In other words, be your own 'coach' and *heal yourself*.

Coupling Up

We have included a chapter on twosomes – not just for the romance of two superb looking people, scantily clad in the privacy of their own pool gym. That's certainly part of it, sure. It's mainly because another body, added to the natural buoyancy of water, not only overcomes any of the limitations (mainly of leverage) that water has for some exercises, but also allows for some outrageously good stretching and flexing exercises.

Since almost anybody can lift almost anybody in water, it's much like being moved around by your own friendly giant.

It's really great fun, too. You couldn't do anything like it on dry land. A little commonsense is needed, but generally coupling exercises in water can lead to almost everything . . . all of which is good!

3
How to Use This Book

Having read the book through and understanding the range of exercises available to you in water, you can make up your own daily-or-so sets of exercises by picking out which ones you want from Chapters 9, 10 and/or 12.

Make sure you regularly vary them to maintain that spice of variety. Also, try to beat the previous time's vigor and repetition and/or distance done.

Try, too, to gradually select the harder routines and to get to carry them out in the most arduous way – as indicated with the suggestions under the notation 'More Difficulty'.

Remember, you are not really as super-fit as you would secretly wish yourself to be unless you can absorb all that the most rigorous routines in this book can throw at you.

Remember, too, that if you have any part of your body you wish to concentrate on, either for better good looks or because of muscular/limb weakness, then go to the appropriate section in Chapter 11.

In these 'anatomical' sections, you will find cross-references in the descriptions of the exercises to other muscle groups or joints that are benefited by the same exercise. So, when you've gone through the routines to, say, improve your buttocks, you can easily find other parts of your body that can be helped by adapting the same exercise in a slightly different way.

For those special water-fitness needs, outside of beauty and body development, look up Chapters 13 and 14.

Finally, an Index gives you a ready interlinkage from any one part of the book to another.

4
Feeling Yourself Feeling Good

The underlying reason to exercise is to not only feel good but to feel healthy in yourself because you're on top of the world in all departments.

You don't quite feel good when you've failed to achieve the goals laid down by someone who presents you with a chart for yesterday, today and tomorrow. Your body might feel okay, but you sense that you've failed a bit. That's not quite feeling good about feeling good; there's a doubt about not really measuring up to par.

That's why you are your own best coach, when it comes to what you should achieve each day. If you're feeling low or justifiably tired or emotionally drained, then it is a superb attainment if you exercise anywhere near yesterday's effort when you were on top of the world. No one but you knows about that.

It is interesting that this selfhood approach is used in most of the open-age swimming competitions that are now all the rage throughout the western world. People of all ages compete in national and international competitions, just as we see at the Olympics. They are up and down the pool just like we see all those young world-beaters do; they are in formal heats, and they race over various distances with different strokes according to their ability.

There's one big and sensible difference. These 'oldies' (which in swimming generally means over 25!) are not competing against each other, but to beat their *own* time. Sure, there are local, national and international records that are official. But if you yourself beat your own best recorded time, you have broken a record nonetheless valid. And that's the basis of the whole affair.

So, if you're going to be your own coach, as it were, you perhaps ought to begin by understanding the simplified basics of what exercise is all about and how you should best go about using this book.

The Aerobic Benefits

Aerobic exercises literally mean those exercises 'with oxygen', as against anaerobic exercises which are those 'without oxygen'. In general terms, aerobic exercises involve movement in unfixed resistances, such as air or water; with these endurance-type exercises, the body gets plenty of oxygen and gets benefits over a long time without a great deal of sudden stress on the heart. Anaerobic exercises involve movement with fixed resistances generally, such as the fixed weights on the end of a barbell; these sharp and brief exercises place much stress on the heart under conditions of oxygen deprivation.

Swimming and water exercising are just about the best kind of activities for good all-round aerobic exercising. You can get as much oxygen as you need over a long period and so get your heart rate up to a beneficial working or training level. Alongside of the muscle and joint benefits you get, this aerobic bonus of water exercising provides a tremendous positive effect for your heart, blood passages and lungs.

Water is so aerobically good because its smoothness imparts even less strain to movement than the other aerobic pursuits like running, cycling, skiing and so forth. Put simply, you don't get so many of those jolts which can briefly turn an aerobic routine into an anaerobic one unexpectedly and unwantedly. This extra 'gentleness' means less strain on the heart, less stress on muscles, less raising of the blood pressure. You're breathing better, because water helps you breathe more deeply, which means that your lungs are processing more oxygen and cleaning out more of those unwanted toxic wastes from your blood stream.

The resulting healthier pounding of your heart is also good for capillary health in your muscles; for your veins and arteries, so they become more resilient and less likely to blockage; for your metabolism; for your self confidence, since you're feeling better and coping better, and are alert, and have more energy during the day.

When you are exercising, learn to listen to your body. One tell-tale for you will be your heart rate. To get a good aerobic training effect from your water exercising, get your heart beat up to a working rate of around 120 beats per minute. This varies between men and women, and between individuals, but you'll be able to tell when it's a healthy thumping after you've been exercising for some time. (If you want to estimate your heart beat rate, place your fingertips on your carotid artery at the base of your throat; count beats for five or ten seconds; then multiply by 12 or 6 to get a per-minute ratio.)

After you are no longer just a novice to water exercising you should aim to keep up your working heart rate for at least 20 minutes, hopefully, a day. When you are just starting up using your pool as a gym, though, take things very easily at first.

Incidentally, many topflight athletes use the pool for anaerobic exercising, too.

A different way of getting fit in water out of your depth — walking through it!

This is especially so if their specialties are in areas of short, concentrated bursts, like sprinters on the track or in the pool, or top squash players. To get these anaerobic 'benefits', they use the pool to swim underwater repeatedly as far as they can, or do sprint laps without breathing, and so on. Some of the more advanced exercises in this book can also be adapted to achieve such training results, if desired.

Exercising

We all know that exercising is better than not exercising and that diet has much to do with a healthy body, exercised or not exercised. The real message behind all today's confusing fitness-science craze is really: *keep on the go; don't let life find you not wriggling.*

To get the best out of that half-hour or so you put aside each day or each other day, it's best to treat your body gently at first.

Around your muscles, bones and joints you've got a blood (or energy) circulating system. So the trick is to get the blood (or energy) gently ticking sweetly around your body first. The best, gentle way of doing this is to do *stretching* exercises which hopefully combine getting the muscles and joints ready for any exercise shock to come with starting the blood pumping.

When you've stretched most of the muscle groups, then you should look to get the heart really primed and the blood even more healthily coursing through your veins with *warm-up* exercises.

Now that your fires have been stoked and all the moving parts oiled, you're ready for developing strength (it helps to cope with the world) and endurance (it also helps to cope with the world) by launching yourself into the *flexing* exercises.

Thus, the pattern you should keep firmly in your mind for when you set your own daily program is:

> stretching exercises, or the stretchers
> warm-up exercises
> flexing exercises, or the flexers

generally in that order. But the essential gentle nature of water can mean that if you want to do a reasonable warm-up exercise first before your stretching routine, then by all means indulge yourself. You might feel just so exuberant that you want to fool around in the water first, or it might be a mite too chilly to remain too static initially.

The Stretchers

Stretching exercises give the major muscles of your body a good wakeup. A good old-fashioned yawn is a prime example of a good old-fashioned stretching exercise. The object is to gradually stretch the various parts of your body one-by-one and, each time, to hold that stretched-out position until you feel that familiar discomfort in the muscle affected. You then 'release' it and do it again for as many times as you think or feel fit.

Your muscles benefit by this naturally-lengthening process – and so do all the connecting tissues to them whether they are tendons (which connect muscle to bone) or ligaments (which connect bone to bone). They benefit for the simple reason that muscles can only expand or contract; if you contract them you'll either end up 'uptight', because that's what happens to them when you're angry or frustrated, or with that body building muscle-bound look, because muscles get chunky that way.

Stretching them, first of all, keeps their range of movement as accommodating of daily needs as possible, to reduce daily soreness and stiffness. Secondly, it allows them to develop in a nice smooth fashion. And it's that smoothness that we associate with good looks.

The stretchers also help the joints go through their paces without overaction. It gets them oiled up for the more vigorous routines.

We have divided the body into five parts:

1 *Legs* – includes thighs, hamstrings, calves, groin, knees, hips, ankles and feet.

2 *Arms* – includes upper and lower arms, shoulder, wrists and hands.

3 *Back* – includes spine, back muscles, buttocks and chest.

4 *Stomach and Chest* – includes abdominal muscles, waist, chest (lungs) and side muscles (laterals).

5 *Neck* – just neck.

A few minutes for each exercise should be enough for you, but you might wish to do more or less. Certainly, though, you should try to do a variety of initial stretching exercises that take in each of the major five of our groupings above. There's plenty of stretchers for you to choose from. They are indicated in the descriptions, of course, as 'Stretchers'.

The Warmers-Up

This is frolic time. As I have mentioned, you can do this either before the stretchers or between the stretchers and the more rigorous flexers. Unlike a lot of advice you'll get, I recommend it between.

Whenever you do it, enjoy, enjoy. If you're a drag-foot type like most of us and were really honest, you'd have to say that the warmer-up is the only time you can really enjoy the regular time (hopefully once a day, but not necessary) that we humans should set aside for exercising.

It's to rev up the motor, now that you've got the contraption oiled up and idling.

All worthy exercising is about avoiding shock to the parts of the body going through their paces – and all warmers-up do is to raise the rate of blood circulation (energy and so forth), prod the heart into a more preparatory rate, warm up your muscles and joints and all that tissue and give you that internal temperature which makes you feel more comfortable if you're losing a bit of heat to surrounding water.

You're now ready to get into the heavy stuff . . . the 'Flexers'.

The Flexers

These exercises, it should be said right off, are here called flexers, because flexing is what muscles must do if they are not strictly stretching. The use of the word is to denote the movement of the muscles, joints, etc, not the so-called *flexibility* that becomes just one attribute of a healthy muscle. We use the terms 'flexers' or 'flexing' exercises in that way, unlike a lot of other fitness proponents.

Now, the flexers are the business end of the engagement of fitness upon you.

They tone the body either generally or specifically, so you can choose what result you want from them. This book helps you do that. Remember, too, that a good deal of water exercises are especially good for the general benefit it gives to so many muscles at any one time.

So the flexers are your tools for gaining from your pool gym the toning effects you really want. Select them according to that or just enjoy the wide range.

You should do your flexing exercises according to what you want out of them. I mentioned earlier that the general thrust of exercising is to gain for yourself endurance, so you should do your selected exercises with a middle-rate vigor but aim to do them for a longer period each time. (If you've half a mind to, that is!)

In our notations, we have used the word 'repetition' to imply to you that an exercise can be made more difficult, as particularly regards endurance, if you repeat it more – that is, put aside longer time for it.

Obviously, there is a lot of overlapping between the four benefits (endurance, strength, resilience and energy loss) you seek to derive from exercises, but in general terms if you wish to increase your strength you should do your exercises with greater vigor. This means really *heaving* as best you can against the water or kicking as strongly against it as you can.

In our notations, we have used the word 'vigor' to indicate this.

If you've worked well at one exercise with either vigor or repetition or (preferably) both, then you're really achieving the right heights if you can go on to the next exercise with a decreasing wait over yesterday or last week or whatever. That's getting to the general fitness that is resilience. We haven't notated that, because only you can gauge that.

And if you've got all three (endurance, strength, resilience) really together, then you'll lose weight in water just as effectively, if not more effectively, than on dry land.

The 'More Difficult' Factor

Water's natural resistance works like weights on an exercise machine, except that these 'weights' are at your fingertip control and have an infinite variety that accords to your wishes. As if those advantages weren't already enough, in water you also have the added facility of moving your weights around anywhere in the pool gym, within standing or floating reason.

For example, if you want to make your running on the spot a more rigorous routine, you can simply move into deeper water. With that extra weight and resistance of water on you, you'll really feel you've been exercising if you try to maintain the same sort of vigor and repetition as you had in the shallower water.

So, your pool gym offers you three basic fingertip-control ways of increasing the difficulty of any exercise:

1 vigor
2 repetition
3 depth of water

There is also a fourth basic: distance. This obviously applies to the mobile exercises, like running, walking or swimming. So, let's add the minority fourth:

4 distance

The Dimensions of Your Pool Gym

Your pool won't be the same as your neighbor's. You'd be upset if it was, probably. There are many shapes and sizes, especially when it comes to the shallowest and the deepest depths and the holding-on facilities. You might have a ladder which is great for the holding-on exercises, or you might have steps, or both. You might have a holding rail around the edges or overlapping tiles, and so forth.

We haven't been able to cover all the various differences in pool design but you'll find that, with a bit of thought, you'll be able to adapt just about every exercise to your pool.

Sometimes you can adapt yourself to the design of your pool gym! For example, if you're wanting to do the Deep Press-Ups exercise, it might be that your deep end isn't deep enough to allow you the full body extension. Okay, simply bend your legs backwards when you are extended. A simple adaptation like that not only makes all possible in your pool gym, but actually makes the exercise more worthily difficult.

5
Water Exercising, Music, Aerobics?

Why not? If your neighbors don't mind, it's really very good to have your portable radio or cassette player on the side of the pool and do your routines to good vibrations.

Music gives added exhilaration and added enjoyment – and therefore, for some, added incentive to exercise. Any incentive like this will certainly translate itself into vigor and benefit, so that's good.

It doesn't have to always be on the upbeat side of frantic, either. A good, soothing classical station or tape can be a most relaxing, almost spiritual way of performing your routines. It might be how you feel on the day. Alternatively, you might just like the chancey nature of the beat of the next record to dictate what rhythm you'll follow for the next water exercise set.

If you're into the more upbeat routine, though, you can indulge yourself to good fitness effect just as much in the pool as you do in your Aerobics class down at your local fitness centre. In fact, with any type of music — whether it be rock, jazz, semi-classical or classical — you can get even better aerobic-exercise benefits in water. You won't get so tired; you will be able to exercise to the music for longer periods without resting; you can adjust the difficulty or the posture of the exercises more fluidly; and you will find that any after effects of tiredness or soreness will be much less after the first few times.

Certainly, the positive effects for you of aerobic exercising (as discussed in the section 'The Aerobic Benefits' in Chapter 4) combined with the sheer sense of release which comes from water will give you many affirmatives as to why water exercising and music do mix — and mix well.

6
Water Exercising and Swimming

The vast majority of exercises given here are for non-swimmers.

That is not to say that, if you are a swimmer, you should scorn water exercising. Far from it. These exercises can be tough for all. What swimmers do have, though, is an expanded range of activities to work with. The activities should be able to re-establish or enhance your communication with the medium you probably love best.

Most of us can swim to some degree. Even if you're only a beginner, I recommend that you end your exercising session with whatever laps you can accomplish.

There is no hard and fast rule about the number of laps you should do or the pace at which you do them. It's just that moving through water exercises at the one time most of the muscle groups of your body; so if you can end your water exercising program with a vigorous lap or two or more, then you're lucky. You have that extra variety.

Bear in mind that water exercises are not a way to teach you how to swim better. They are a way to allow you to get fit better. Being a swimmer is an added advantage, that's all.

You'll be able to say, 'I can't swim very well, but my pool has made me really fit'. Wouldn't that be a nice turn-up? It's so easily achievable too.

See also Chapter 10.

────7────
Water Exercising and the Cold

If you don't live in the tropics or have a heated pool, there'll be months of the year in which your pool gym will seem unfriendly.

Even if that's so, you'll still be using a superb fitness medium for much of the year. Apart from the emotional aspect of water seeming too cold to go in, you should think about it a little longer. Even on dry land it's pretty uncomfortable getting going in cold weather, but, once you start, it all becomes very much more comfortable. The same generally goes for a pool gym.

Water exercising, believe me, is vigorous at its very basics, so you'll get very quickly all the heat generation you will need.

Get a good idea of the routine you want to perform and, contrary to what most experts will tell you, you will find that the heat loss to water is refreshing, not debilitating, in all but the most arctic of waters.

Mind you, this is not to deny that there is an initial shock of entering water in coolish to cold temperatures. You can shake yourself around to get the circulation flowing before you enter if you wish. You can grit your teeth and get the stimulation of that initial shiver (you can get hooked on that 'pleasant' experience – and colds have nothing to do with it *per se*).

Wet Suits!

Alternatively, you can invest a little money and buy a lightweight wet suit which is very light, sleeveless and only covers the torso. You can even use a heavyweight wet suit. It's only water clothing, after all. And it allows you to exercise without that loss of body heat you might think unpleasant.

Surfers use lightweight and heavyweight wet suits to enjoy their sport the year round. Divers do the same. Triathlon athletes use lightweight wet suits during competition. So it's commonsense – and not expensive commonsense – to do the same in order to utilise that great gym medium you have out back.

It's all up to you, and that's the nice thing about having your own gym facility close by.

The other obvious avenue is there for you too: during those cold months you keep up your water exercise routines down at your neighborhood or club heated pool.

8

Helpful Devices for the Super-fit and Not-so-fit

A kick board is one of the more useful aids for you.

Wearing one or both swim fins or flippers is undoubtedly the best way of strengthening lower-half muscles. You will find it quite amazing how much extra effort you need to put into a leg movement if you have a swim fin on your foot.

Just try the Sideswiping exercise (number 23) with a flipper on your outside leg. There's real muscle power needed.

Alternatively, if you ever want to dispel an acquaintance's scepticism about the potential ruggedness of water exercising, just get them to try Sideswiping with a swim fin on. And Sideswiping is one of the easiest leg exercises.

Doing your flotation and swimming exercises with swim fins increases benefit, as well. The flipper's broader reaction against water resistance allows you to maintain a better balance and rhythm and this allows you to put more into your routine.

Swim fins are cheap, too. So are hand paddles. They are simple plastic 'slabs' that slip on to your hands and wrists – and they have the same benefits for your torso and upper body as swim fins do for your lower body.

As with Sideswiping with swim fins, try Fanning (numbers 4, 5 or 6) with hand paddles.

With swim fins and hand paddles you can go for the real chunky body building look to your thighs, buttocks, calves, chest, shoulders, arms. They are real tools that don't hurt the pocket.

There are other devices – like kick boards, pull buoys, old shoes or boots, an object held in the hand to give added weight, 'octopus rope' for the feet, water wings, and so forth – that are part of a training swimmer's apparatus. By all means use them, if you want to. You'll have a lot of fun experimenting with how to use them in the most effective ways and in more varied routines.

Certainly, the floating devices (the kick board, the buoys, even an improvised auto tyre tube) can help you or one of your loved ones. This might be needed because of soreness or being worried about people getting out of their depth. So they can be useful to have around.

Some people always use a cap and swim goggles whenever they go in. It might look a bit like they're going out to swim the English Channel, but they feel more comfortable that way. And that's good. Certainly swim goggles are recommended.

There is one other improvisation you can do that isn't the gimmick it might seem to be at first sight. If you have a plastic or fibreglass (ie, non-rusting) coffee table or small bench, then put it in your pool so that its top is less than a foot below the surface of the water. When you lay on it on your back or on your front, you will easily keep it steady enough by holding on to its sides. This will open up all those exercises that you could do if you were lying on a dryland gym bench – such as (on your back) tucking your knees into your chest but letting your legs stretch far below the horizontal in the start position; or (on your front; neck back and face out of the water, of course!) arching back while flinging arms and legs out wide.

It's your gym. Do what you like in it.

═══9═══

The Exercises
Easy-to-Intermediate Levels

The exercises in this section are loosely arranged in recommended order. The easiest exercises are at the beginning of the section; the more difficult at the end. With the stretching exercises, remember to stretch the muscles slowly. Do not jerk or lunge initially. You will often read in the instructions: 'Hold for a good stretch'. This means you should keep in the extreme position until you feel the muscle getting the benefit of being stretched. This could also mean feeling trembling or slight pain. Until you get either of these, you won't be benefiting from the exercise.

We don't give any hard-and-fast rule about how long you should hold any one position or how many times you should repeat any one exercise. You are the best judge of your own body. You work it out.

If you want to keep a chart and compete with that in some way each time, all well and good.

Remember: Get a breathing pattern. Exhale on action phase. Inhale on relaxation phase.

JOY OF SPRING
Warm-up/flexer
Standing
Benefits: general body
(especially thighs, ankles,
stomach, shoulders)

In at least waist-depth, jump repeatedly and 'joyously' in any or all directions. Make sure you fling out arms when at top of jump; also keep your stomach muscles taut. Start leisurely and get more vigorous until you are doing it exhilaratingly. Done before the stretchers, it will take the chill out of the water for you during cooler weather.

More Difficulty:
1. vigor and repetition;
2. use as a mainstream flexing exercise, just before Running (q.v.);
3. move to deeper water (up to chest depth) and try to jump as high out of water as possible without losing balance.

CALF STRETCH
Stretcher
Standing
Benefits: calves, hamstrings, small of back, shoulders, wrists

In chest depth or less, lean against side of pool, arms outstretched and body at approx. 45 degrees to bottom. Keeping feet flat on bottom, lean into wall, arms bending. Keep back straight and lean as far as your chin touching the side. Hold for good stretch along back of legs. Return to starting position, then repeat as required.

More Difficulty:
1. longer hold and repetition;
2. stand on one leg and repeat exercise, then change legs.

STORCH STRETCH
Stretcher
Standing
Benefits: front thigh, ankles, back

In minimum waist-depth, bend one knee backwards and bring foot up to same-side hand. Pull on leg to tuck heel into buttocks is possible. Hold for good stretch of front thigh while keeping back straight and shoulder blades together. Repeat as required. Then do exercise with other leg.

More Difficulty:
1. longer hold and repetition.

FRONT FANNING
Flexer
Standing
Benefits: chest, back, shoulders, arms

(Note: with this and with all water exercises, the best benefit is gained if you use your palms as oars – that is, each time you sweep your arms through the water, turn your palms into the direction the arms are going. This way, they 'cup' the water and allow you to control greater resistance.)
In shoulder-depth water or kneeling so that water comes up to shoulders, extend arms together in front of you, then pull back to maximum open-arms position. Try to get your shoulder blades to meet and keep hands and fingers outstretched. Repeat as required.

More Difficulty:
1. pull harder through water, plus repetition.

FANNING BENEATH
Flexer
Standing
Benefits: chest, back, shoulders, arms

In belly-depth, so that when you bend over at 90 degrees, your face is just out of the water, and from the arms outstretched together 'beneath' you, heave upwards to your maximum possible open-arms position. Don't forget to use palms as oars by turning them to face the direction your arms are moving in. Keep your arms and back straight, and hands and fingers outstretched. You are doing exercise very well if your arms come out of water above you.

More Difficulty:
1. pull harder upwards and downwards through water, plus repetition.

FANNING VERTICALLY
Flexer
Standing
Benefits: chest, side muscles, shoulders, arms

In shoulder-depth when either standing or kneeling (if pool isn't deep enough), start with arms stretched down at the sides, chest out, stomach in, back upright. Using palms as oars to cup water each way, pull arms upwards to surface of water, then lower again to sides. Keep back straight, chest out.

More Difficulty:
1. vigor, plus repetition;
2. continue with upwards swing of arms until they are
· extended above head with hands and fingers stretched upwards.

FAN AND HEAVE
Flexer
Standing
Benefits: chest, side muscles, shoulders

Do previous exercise (Fanning Vertically), but when arms are extended sideways, just below the surface of the water, turn palms rearwards and heave arms against water to maximum horizontal open-arms position. Try to touch shoulder blades if possible. Heave arms forwards again to sideways extension, then complete previous exercise.

More Difficulty:
1. vigor, plus repetition.

BEACON 1
Flexer
Standing
Benefits: waist, side muscles, thighs, knees

In at least midriff-depth and from a stance of legs comfortably apart with hands on hips, swivel your torso from right to left swinging chest through 180 degrees, if possible. Repeat from side to side, keeping legs straight, and with stomach in and chest out as much as possible. Also keep elbows back at all times.

More Difficulty:
1. vigor, plus repetition.
2. deeper water, up to shoulder depth or until you begin to 'float' off balance.

BEACON 2
Flexer
Standing
Benefits: waist, side muscles, thighs, knees, arms

Do previous exercise (Beacon 1), but instead of hands on hips use arms extended sideways and turning palms as oars with each change of arm direction. The 'front' arm can swing in a greater arc to across the chest if required. *Heave* arms to and fro in water.

More Difficulty:
1. vigor, plus repetition.

RAINBOW
Stretcher or Flexer
Standing
Benefits: side muscles, waist, neck, shoulders, arms

In at least waist-depth with legs comfortably apart and arms hanging down at sides, lean torso to one side while pulling outside arm upwards through water through an arc to swing across head. Proceed to maximum sideways curve of torso and upper arm. Hold there for good stretch if the exercise is being used as a stretching one, or return almost immediately to upright position if exercise is being used as a flexing one. Repeat by leaning to other side as far as is possible. Remember to keep your arms and back as straight as possible, and to use your palms as oars to cup water in each arm direction.

More Difficulty:
1. vigor, plus repetition;
2. deeper water up to shoulder-depth or until you start to feel yourself off balance;
3. do with both arms raised together, starting from arms extended above you and keeping arms swinging in arc together.

RAINBOW CIRCLE
Standing
Flexer
Benefits: side muscles, waist, back, shoulders, neck, arms

In at least chest-depth with arms extended above your head and feet apart comfortably, sway both arms together and torso sideways to maximum lean. Hold for half-stretch, then dip both hands close together into water and, with palms facing in the arm movement direction as oars, pull arms back across body as far as they will go. You will then be turned to face the other direction with arms extended together. Bring back through air to overhead turning back to face front. Instead of stopping here keep arc going to return to maximum lean again, then return arms back through water, etcetera. Change from clockwise to counterclockwise sweeping of arms as required.

More Difficulty:
1. vigor, plus repetition;
2. deeper water and really heave arms through water.

ARM ROUNDERS
Standing
Flexer
Benefits: shoulders, arms, chest

In shoulder-depth, start from position of arms extended out in front. Using palms as oars, pull arms through the water to maximum open-arms position, trying to touch shoulder blades if possible. Here, circle stiff arms in unison in tight circles as though you are stirring up the water. Return arms through water to front extension position. Repeat as desirable.

More Difficulty:
1. vigor, plus repetition;
2. when circling, change from clockwise to counterclockwise in mid-routine.

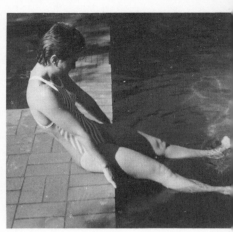

DANGLE ROUNDERS
Stretcher or Flexer
Sitting
Benefits: feet and ankles, thighs, stomach, hips, calves

Sit on side of pool with legs dangling into water and hands holding on to edge. Point toes, then twirl ankles in a circular motion in the water. Do one foot at a time, then both feet together for as long as required Be conscious of keeping toes pointed as much as possible.

More Difficulty:
1. vigor, plus repetition;
2. circle ankles as above, but do so while holding legs stretched out horizontally, keeping them parallel to surface of water;
3. with legs either dangling in the water or stretched above it, pause after circling ankles, 'cocking' feet upwards as far as possible. Hold for good calves stretch.

DANGLE KICK
Flexer
Sitting
Benefits: knee, thighs, feet and ankles, calves, buttocks

Sit on edge of pool holding on to side with legs dangling into water. Keeping back straight and toes pointed, pull legs through water up to surface. Lower to starting position and repeat as necessary, using variations of one leg after the other if you wish.

More Difficulty:
1. vigor (especially with forcing tops of feet through water on upwards push), plus repetition;
2. use swim fins.

BUTTOCK ROLL
Flexer
Sitting
Benefits: buttocks, thighs, feet and ankles, stomach

Either sitting on pool step or in shallow water or (if too deep to keep balance) sitting on the very side of pool, reclining on your bottom with legs outstretched into the water and arms supporting you behind, rock from one side to another as far as possible. Keep stomach in and toes pointed. Make sure that your legs stay in the air to keep good stretch tension on your buttocks while they are 'kneaded' with the rocking.

More Difficulty:
1. vigor, plus repetition.

SIDE ROLL
Stretcher or Flexer
Sitting
Benefits: thighs, upper arms, side muscles, feet and ankles

Either sitting on pool step or in shallow water or (if too deep to keep balance) sitting on the very edge of pool with legs outstretched into the water and with your weight supported by your arms. Take full weight on arms and lift hips off bottom or side, then swing one leg over the other while twisting your body sideways as far as possible. Keep toes pointed and hold for good stretch; or alternatively twist from this side to that in good rhythm.

More Difficulty:
1. vigor, plus repetition;
2. use swim fins for extra benefit to thighs.

HALF PRESS-UPS
Flexer
Standing
Benefits: arms, back, shoulders

In at least hip-depth, position your feet and angle your body so that when you lean against pool wall your arms are extended at a downward angle from you. Ideal position is with your legs forming 45 degrees with the bottom of the pool and your arms 90 degrees with your body when you are leaning against the wall with arms extended. Then do press-ups against wall keeping feet stationary and back as straight as possible. Lean right through until shoulder blades touch if possible and push off until arms are locked straight again. Repeat as required.

More Difficulty:
1. vigor, plus repetition;
2. in chest-depth, so that arms are parallel with surface of water, providing greater water resistance against your chest and back muscles.

GROIN FLEX 1
Stretcher or Flexer
Standing
Benefits: groin, upper thigh, hamstrings

In at least waist-depth with legs comfortably apart, transfer your weight as far over to one side as possible. Keep outside leg straight as possible and hold for good stretch of groin (of outside leg) and thigh (of inside leg). Return slowly to central position, then transfer weight likewise to other side. Repeat as required. If using as flexing exercise, get up good smooth rhythm *but* start slowly. *Note*: holding on to side with one hand and doing exercise facing wall gives excellent added balance either to beginners' or advanced routines.

More Difficulty:
1. repetition;
2. deeper water.

GROIN FLEX 2
Stretcher or Flexer
Standing
Benefits: groin, thigh, hamstring, side muscles, buttocks

In at least chest-depth and with arms extended sideways, raise one knee out to the side and as high as possible. Try to touch arm with knee, but keep your back straight and keep facing to the front. Repeat as required. Then do exercise with other knee.

More Difficulty:
1. vigor, plus repetition;
2. when leg is in highest position, straighten it out as much as possible and try to touch your hand with your toes. Hold for good stretch.

BACK SWALLOW 1
**Stretcher or Flexer
Standing
Benefits:** back, arms, thighs, neck

Brace feet against bottom and side wall, holding on to side with arms extended. Arch back and strain against arms and legs by throwing head back as far as possible. Hold for good stretch or repeat for strong flexing exercise.

More Difficulty:
1. vigor, plus repetition;
2. depth of water.

WATER SPLITS
**Stretcher or Flexer
Standing
Benefits:** groin, thighs, knees

Face side and hold on with hands apart. Take weight on arms and gradually spread legs to good stretched position depending on your suppleness. Then steadily lower yourself (keeping your balance under control with your grip) to extend splits. While in fully extended position, gently bounce up and down. Pull yourself back to starting position and repeat.

More Difficulty:
1. repetition;
2. deeper water as practicable;
3. do free-standing with arms outstretched in front of you (*note*: do this in minimum chest-depth in case slippery bottom causes injury).

SHALLOW BOXING
Flexer
Standing
Benefits: arms, shoulders, waist

Either in shoulder-depth or bending over so surface is at shoulder level, punch out with fist straight in front of you to fully extended arm position, then pull arm back to extreme elbow bent position. Alternate arms vigorously. Remember to keep arms going to full extension even when getting tired.

More Difficulty:
1. vigor, plus repetition;
2. in mid-routine, change to punching arms through a 180-degree arc from one side of your body to the other. Keep up the fanning motion from this side to that side and back again. Maintain rhythm.

SIDESWIPING 1
Stretcher or Flexer
Standing
Benefits: thighs, hamstrings, buttocks, hips, back, feet and ankles

Holding on to side turned sideways or free-standing, push straight leg (with toes pointing all the time) forwards to maximum water-surface height, then swing straight back through arc to elevated rear leg position. Hold at extreme positions for good stretch or repeat as to-and-fro exercise.

More Difficulty:
1. vigor, plus repetition;
2. deeper water up to shoulder-depth, so that you swing leg frontwards up to shoulder height.

BALLET STRETCH
Stretcher
Standing
Benefits: hamstring, back, side muscles, feet and ankles

Place heel on side of pool while standing in at least hip-depth, then reach forward as far as possible along outstretched leg, hopefully to toes and beyond. Keep both legs straight as possible and cock upper foot so that you feel good hamstring stretch when holding. Repeat as often as desired, then change legs.

More Difficulty:
1. longer hold, plus repetition;
2. deeper water.

WATER SQUATS 1
Flexer
Standing
Benefits: legs, buttocks, back

In desired depth, squat on haunches then raise yourself to standing. Keep arms outstretched in front of you or to the side and repeat as necessary.

More Difficulty:
1. vigor, plus repetition;
2. deeper water as practicable;
3. when squatting, point knees as far out to sides as possible, not straight ahead.

WATER SQUATS 2
Flexer
Standing
Benefits: legs, buttocks, back, shoulders

In desired depth, hold on to side with extended arm and turn sideways. Stand on one leg. Using outside arm as balance, repeat Water Squats 1 exercise on one leg only. Repeat as possible then change legs by turning right around.

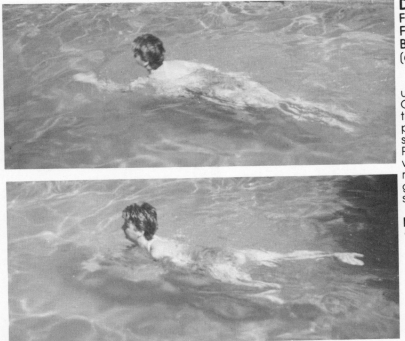

DOG PADDLING
Flexer
Floating
Benefits: general body (especially legs and arms)

Swimming face down but using strokes like a dog would. Concentrate on pulling arms through water as hard as possible and try to heave your shoulders out of water as you go Push arms as far forwards in water as you can, pull through right up to your side. Maintain good rhythm of stroke. Use as sprint, not duration exercise.

More Difficulty:
1. vigor, plus distance.

CHEST PUFFING
Stretcher or Flexer
Sitting
Benefits: back, stomach, upper arms, thighs, chest

In shallows or with arm on a step (and feet on pool bottom), lie face upwards, supporting weight on your arms out behind you. Legs are extended, feet together, toes pointing. Throw back head, throw out chest and arch back. Hold for good stretch of stomach muscles. Repeat.

More Difficulty:
1. vigor, plus repetition.

HURDLING
Flexer
Standing
Benefits: thighs, groin, buttocks, hip

In at least waist-depth, face sideways to wall and hold on with one hand. Raise outside leg to highest position possible behind you, toe pointing and back kept straight. Bring leg forward in an arc as though you are jumping an athletic hurdle. When at most forward position, return leg in same hurdling arc to rear again. Keep toes pointing and back straight at all times. Repeat. Turn around and do with other leg.

More Difficulty:
1. vigor, plus repetition;
2. deeper water;
3. when bring leg around, raise knee as high as it will go until you feel slight discomfort in hip.

WATER DISCO 1
Warm-up or Flexer
Standing
Benefits: general body
(especially waist and
stomach, thighs, side
muscles)

Get up a sort of dancing
movement by twisting whole
torso and right arm to left when
raising left knee as high as
possible, alternating torso and
left arm to right when raising
right knee. Repeat as feels good
for you – from slow, steady
alternating to almost running on
spot. Wonderful exercise to
music. Concentrate on
accentuating knee lift and body
twist. Vary with same leg and
same side torso twist.

More Difficulty:
1. vigor, plus repetition;
2. deeper water, trying to
   maintain same 'pace';
3. shoulder-depth, where your
   arms have to come back
   through the water; this will slow
   down your rhythm but will
   increase strength benefit of
   exercise.

WATER DISCO 2
Warm-up or Flexer
Standing
Benefits: general body
(especially waist and
stomach, thighs, side
muscles)

Perform exercise as Water
Disco 1 (previous), but push legs
out in front of you, knees slightly
bent, as though you were goose-
stepping as part of a lively
dance.

More Difficulty:
1. vigor, plus repetition;
2. deeper water, trying to
   maintain the same 'pace';
3. shoulder-depth, where your
   arms must move through the
   water and you will need much
   more strength to keep up
   anywhere near the same
   pace.

CORKSCREW
Stretcher or Flexer
Standing
Benefits: feet and ankles,
thighs, back

Holding on to side or free-
standing with hands on hips,
extend one leg out sideways.
Point toes for good foot stretch,
then circle foot, both clockwise
and counterclockwise. Keep
back straight.

More Difficulty:
1. vigor, plus repetition.

KICKING IN PLACE 1
Flexer
Floating/holding
Benefits: legs, feet and ankles, side muscles, stomach, shoulders, hips. Also spine (butterfly kick), groin (breaststroke)

Hold on to side with arms outstretched and floating face downwards. Hold head up to breathe and do the following with as much vigor yet control as possible:
1. the freestyle kick, making conscious effort to keep toes pointed and feet turned inwards for best fin effect;
2. the butterfly kick, keeping feet and knees together, toes pointed, and concentrate on small of back moving freely in concert with feet; kick from hips down;
3. the breaststroke kick, move legs parallel to water, keeping feet cocked and giving full knee extension when kicking backwards; make semi-circle when kicking back.

More Difficulty:
1. vigor, plus duration of kicking;
2. breathing from side to side and blowing air out in water;
3. use swim fins.

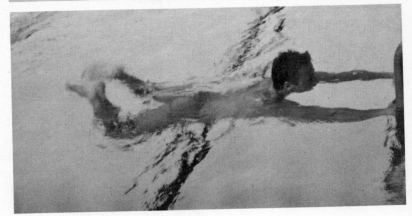

KICKING IN PLACE 2
Flexer
Floating/holding
Benefits: groin, stomach, arms, hips, feet and ankles

Hold on to side with arms bent in locked position so you can keep position steady; face down and legs extended, toes pointing. Kick in a circular motion as though riding a bike. Try to keep as much of kick below water as possible.

More Difficulty:
1. vigor, plus repetition.

SCISSORS
Stretcher or Flexer
Floating/holding
Benefits: groin, inner thighs, stomach, side muscles, feet and ankles

Holding on to side extended face downwards, body and arms stretched out, open legs horizontally as wide as possible, keeping toes pointed and legs straight. Bring legs together again. Repeat as required for either stretching or flexing exercise.

More Difficulty:
1. vigor, plus repetition; or stretch time.

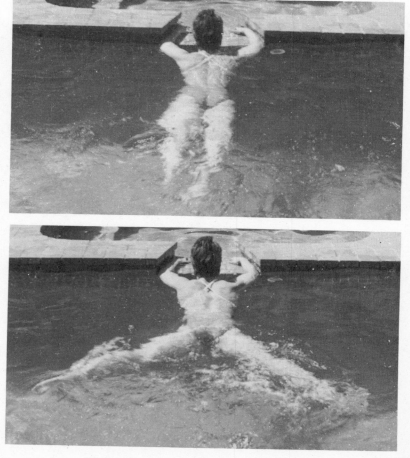

BACK TUCK
Flexer
Floating/holding
Benefits: back, stomach, buttocks, shoulders, thighs, feet and ankles

You have to get a strong grip on the side for this exercise, so, face upwards and with your back to wall, extend your arms along the side or hold pool ladder above your head or improvise similar. Stretch legs outwards with toes pointing. Hold for good stretch of thighs and front of lower leg, then vigorously jack knife your knees up into your chest. Hold for good buttock and stomach stretch, then return legs as slowly as possible. Repeat.

More Difficulty:
1. vigor, plus repetition.

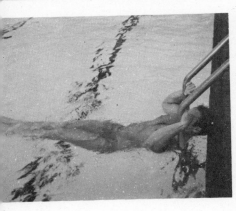

BACK SCISSORS WITH TUCK
Flexer
Floating/holding
Benefits: back, groin, buttocks, thighs, shoulders, feet and ankles

Holding on to side or pool ladder, floating stretched out on back, as in exercise Back Tuck. Perform Scissors routine (35) opening legs as far as possible, return legs together to central position, then vigorously jack knife your knees up into your chest. Lower legs to outstretch as slowly as possible, then repeat scissors movement, followed by knees tuck again, etcetera.

More Difficulty:
1. vigor, plus repetition.

38

JACK KNIFE
Flexer
Floating/holding
Benefits: back, stomach, hamstrings, buttocks, shoulders.

Arms along side or holding ladder above head, on back, body stretched out, feet together, toes pointing. Keeping legs straight, raise them first to vertical, then to over your head as far as possible. Do this by curling your back and using your shoulders as leverage. Hold as long as possible in extreme position, then return legs to outstretch in water as slowly as possible. Repeat.

More Difficulty:
1. vigor, plus repetition.

39

PUSH AND PULL
Flexer
Floating/holding
Benefits: upper arms, side muscles, neck, spine

Extend your arms in front of you and hold on to side with good grip. Use a small kick to float your body away from wall. *Note*: if necessary, keep a small kick going throughout this exercise to keep afloat. Pull vigorously against wall to haul body in, then push against wall to push body out. Repeat.

More Difficulty:
1. vigor, plus repetition;
2. do with one arm holding side, other arm keeping balance.

REVERSE SCISSORS
Flexer
Floating/holding
Benefits: groin, stomach, shoulders, buttocks, feet and ankles

With back to wall and floating face upwards, hold on to side as best you can to maintain float. Stretch legs out together and, keeping toes pointed, open legs as wide as possible. Hold for good stretch, then move feet in small circles; many as possible. Return to starting position and repeat.

More Difficulty:
1. vigor, plus repetition.

ONE-ARM PADDLE
Flexer
Floating/holding
Benefits: arms, side muscles, stomach, shoulders

Hold on to side with one hand, keeping body stretched and face down by kicking slightly. Free hand is then pulled vigorously forwards towards wall using palm turned to cup water. Keep holding arm stiff to get benefit of resistance. When free arm completes forward stroke, pull backwards with palm turned to cup water as oar. Again use other arm as brace. Try to keep your body stationary as possible during exercise; this will rely on the strength of your holding arm. Repeat rapidly. Change over arms.

More Difficulty:
1. vigor, plus repetition.

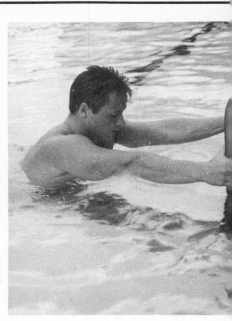

WALL SHOVE
Flexer
Floating/holding
Benefits: back, hamstrings, calves, knees, arms, thighs, feet and ankles

Arms half-locked, hold on to side with feet placed against side wall. Then tuck in your head, extend arms and straighten legs as much as possible by pushing out your rear-end. Hold for good strain. Relax. Bring feet back to brace against wall. Repeat.

More Difficulty:
1. vigor, plus repetition;
2. place feet higher up wall so they are nearer your hands;
3. widen distance between your hands.

PUSH, PULL AND SHOVE
Flexer
Floating/holding
Benefits: general body (especially back, hamstrings, spine, upper arms, stomach)

Hold on to side, arms half-locked and feet on side wall as in previous exercise. Pull in towards wall sharply, kicking legs out behind you. Immediately push arms out to extend. You are now in a face-down, floating position. Hold. Take deep breath, heave in on arms and bring legs sharply back to wall in a half-circular (breaststroke-type) motion. When there, straighten both arms and legs as much as possible as if trying to shove wall away from you. Hold. Push feet out from wall again, etcetera. Repeat movements as a rhythmic exercise.

More Difficulty:
1. vigor, plus repetition;
2. when legs stretched out behind you, do scissors.

SHIP ROLL
Flexer
Floating/holding
Benefits: shoulders, waist, back, feet and ankles

Arms along side or holding pool ladder above head, hold body outstretched, face upwards, legs together and toes pointing. Swivel whole body to the right and left in as wide an arc as possible.

More Difficulty:
1. vigor, plus repetition;
2. bend knees at each swivel; keep knees together;
3. perform swivel as right leg swinging over to left, left leg over to right and so forth.

RUNNING ON SPOT
Warm-up/Flexer
Standing
Benefits: legs, hips, buttocks, feet and ankles

In at least waist-depth, run on spot, accentuating the knee-up movement. Try to get knees to surface of water. Repeat as many times as benefits.

More Difficulty:
1. vigor, plus repetition;
2. deeper water, up to chest-depth, bringing knees up to as high as you can or water allows, while maintaining 'pace';
3. See Sprint (Exercise 58).

ASTRIDE JUMPING
Warm-up/Flexer
Standing
Benefits: groin, buttocks, hips, thighs

In at least waist-depth, stand with legs comfortably apart and hands on hips. Jump to bring legs together. Keep hands on hips at all times. Repeat as continuous exercise.

More Difficulty:
1. vigor, plus repetition;
2. deeper water, trying to maintain same jumping frequency.

HOPPING MAD 1
Warm-up/Flexer
Standing
Benefits: thighs, calves, ankles, buttocks

Holding on to side while facing it or standing free, jump vigorously from one foot to another. Best in just above waist-depth. Keep chest 'puffed' out at all times. Use arms leverage to give good bounce.

More Difficulty:
1. vigor, plus repetition;
2. deeper water, trying to maintain pace.

HOPPING ON SPOT
Flexer
Standing
Benefits: hips, thighs, ankles, stomach, back

Hop on spot on both legs in at least waist-depth. Try to keep back as straight as possible, together with chest out and stomach in.

More Difficulty:
1. vigor, plus repetition;
2. deeper water, maintaining same pace;
3. jump higher, especially in deeper water;
4. hop on one leg, varying 1, 2, and 3 above.

HOPPING MAD 2
Warm-up/Flexer
Standing
Benefits: thighs, calves, hamstrings, groin, buttocks

In waist-depth with hands on hips and standing free, hop from one foot to another. Without breaking rhythm, change to kicking each foot out in front. When ready, change to kicking each foot out to side as far as possible. Return to straight hopping, then repeat routine.

More Difficulty:
1. vigor, plus repetition;
2. deeper water to chest-depth.

PORPOISING 1
Flexer
Standing/immersing
Benefits: general body (especially thighs, side muscles, shoulders, lungs, stomach)

In at least waist-depth, extend arms out in front and dive in a graceful arc to the bottom in front of you. Touch bottom with hands, take weight on arms, transfer weight to legs and kick off bottom forwards so that you break surface in the middle of an arc on way to loop-diving to bottom again. Repeat sequence and progress along pool. Take deep breath as you break the surface and blow out all air in your lungs (make a lot of bubbles!) during the time your are underwater.

More Difficulty:
1. vigor, plus repetition;
2. distance you travel around pool;
3. deeper water, in which you spring as high as you can off bottom to break surface in an impressive 'porpoise' loop.

SQUAT JUMPS
Flexer
Standing
Benefits: calves, thighs, hips, buttocks, chest, shoulders

In at least waist-depth, squat on haunches, arms extended either out front or sideways, spring upwards as high as you can while keeping balanced and raising arms to outstretch above your head. Repeat to good rhythm. Keep your outstretched arms above water surface at all times, or you will over-balance.

More Difficulty:
1. vigor, plus repetition.

FEET FIRST SCULLING
Flexer
Floating
Benefits: arms, stomach, shoulders, feet and ankles

Float on back with feet together and legs extended. Keeping legs still, use hands in a figure-of-eight fashion but down at your sides to propel you feet-first. Look at toes to keep body slightly bent. When required, reverse hand movement, turning palms to cup the water as appropriate, and propel yourself head-first. Keep legs still and toes pointed at all times.

More Difficulty:
1. vigor, plus repetition;
2. use breaststroke pulls with arms, pulling through to maximum front and rear positions.

10

The Exercises

Intermediate-to-Advanced levels

These exercises are for the fit to super-fit. You can't be too unhealthy if you can do these with a smile on your face.

Mind you, you don't have to be a swimmer at all, let alone a good swimmer, to do the great majority of these exercises in this Section. You need only be 'not easily drownable' to benefit from these advanced routines. That's why we've used the notations 'Floating' and 'Floating/holding' and so on to describe the postures.

The only thing you must do is remember that you will always bob back up to the surface. I'm not being alarmist about the dangers of these exercises, because there's really very little danger in them for anyone 'not easily drownable'. All I'm saying is that if you remember and keep reminding yourself that you will always bob back up to the surface again sooner or later (and much sooner than later), then you'll start relaxing even if you can barely swim.

When you start relaxing, then you'll start to do your routines with style and flair and rhythm. And once you get that approach, you'll be reaping marvellous pleasure from playing around in water as well as marvellous fitness benefits.

When you are exercising while floating, breathing itself stretches the rib cage and does wonders for your lungs. Like lap-swimming, too, floating water exercises give benefits over most of your muscles and joints. It's water's superb flotation-but-tension factor about which we've spoken previously. That is why this Section has more of the seemingly-vaguer notation 'General Body' than in the previous Section. In these cases, if you want special benefit to one part of your anatomy or other (say, bigger triceps or so), then it's up to you to emphasise that part of your movements. You can work on the part that benefits you most wantedly as well as getting a great general body workout. That's what's so great about water. Even the simple act of staying afloat is a pretty energetic exercise.

Do It Just as Good

If you are a swimmer, these more advanced routines can be done before or after your lap swimming. They'll give your training variety and increase your pool pleasure.

But if you're not a lap swimmer, they can be used in place of doing laps. In fact, just because you're not a swim-meet Olympian doesn't mean that you're going to do these more advanced exercises any less well than that swim-meet Olympian next door. With these exercises, you can look just as good as him or her and get as much bodily benefits out of water exercising as he or she gets out of ploughing up and down lanes at a rate of knots.

The thing to do is to take your time, concentrate on doing the routines with a combination of strength and rhythm, and keep remembering to breathe in and out with unhurried confidence. You'll get as fit and as poolworthy as that gold medal winner over the fence.

Think of the admiring looks you'll get around the hotel pool during the next vacation.

Remember: Get a breathing pattern. Exhale on action phase. Inhale on relaxation phase.

PADDLE FANNING
Flexer
Standing
Benefits: arms, back, shoulders, chest, stomach

Using hand paddles, do the following exercises:
Front Fanning (Exercise 4)
Fanning Beneath (Exercise 5)
Fanning Vertically (Exercise 6)
Keep up the rhythm of changing from one exercise to the other and really *heave* arms through water.

More Difficulty:
1. vigor, plus repetition;
2. adapt water depth to strain exercising to utmost benefit.

CANOEING
Warm-up/Flexer
Standing
Benefits: arms, side muscles, waist, legs

Like Water Disco 1 (Exercise 30) but this time you use both arms together as you would use a single paddle in a canoe, sweeping past your body in an upwards to downwards sweep and ending well to the rear of you. At the same time you should lift your same-side knee (ie, left knee when arms are going to end sweep on left side) to get good body pull. Do exercise in ideally mid-chest depth and get up a paddling rhythm. Really heave arms through water.

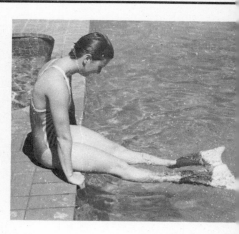

DANGLE KICK 2
Flexer
Sitting
Benefits: knees, thighs, feet and ankles

Sit on edge of pool dangling legs in water *wearing swim fins*, then lift one leg to horizontal position, pulling upwards through water to gain benefit of flipper on your foot. Lower leg back to dangle by similarly forcing leg down against water resistance. Repeat with same leg as required. Then change legs.

More Difficulty:
1. vigor, plus repetition;
2. repeat exercise routine using both legs at the same time.

BACK SWALLOW 2
Stretcher or Flexer
Holding
Benefits: back, shoulders, chest, thighs, neck

Brace feet against side wall in out-of-depth water, holding on to side with arms extended in front of you. Gain rapid purchase on wall with your toes and, at same time, throw back your head and arch your back. Strain against arms and legs as you keep them straight. Hold for good stretch or repeat as flexing exercise.

SIDESWIPING 2
Flexer
Standing/holding
Benefits: thighs, hamstrings, buttocks, calves, back, feet and ankles

Repeat Sideswiping 1 (Exercise 23) of swinging leg back and forwards to maximum front and rear heights while holding on to side, but wear a swim fin on outside leg. Ensure you use arm leverage and taut stomach muscles to swing leg through maximum water resistance you can 'apply' to yourself.

SPRINT
Flexer
Standing
Benefits: general body (especially thighs, calves, waist, feet and ankles)

Instead of running on spot, change to sprinting as fast as you can go on spot in at least waist-depth. This will be difficult to do unless you 'fight' against the viscosity of the water and force yourself to do sharp and vigorous stomping steps – hence the exercise's benefit.

HANGMAN'S KICK 1
Flexer
Holding
Benefits: arms, shoulders, side muscles, thighs, groin, hip

With front to the wall, hang from side or from pool ladder in out-of-depth water. Dangle from arms with feet together and toes pointing. Keeping torso as still as possible, swing one leg to the side as far as possible. Hold as necessary, then return to central position. Keep toes pointed at all times. Repeat with one leg after the other, or do routine as one-leg exercises followed by other-leg exercises.

More Difficulty:
1. vigor, plus repetition;
2. shallower (yes!) water, where you have to tuck your legs up behind you to avoid standing on bottom;
3. use swim fin.

HANGMAN'S KICK 2
Flexer
Holding
Benefits: arms, shoulders, side muscles, thigh, groin, hip, neck

Do previous exercise (Hangman's Kick 1) routine, but do so while *back* to side wall. Greater benefit will be felt in shoulders and neck in order to keep torso 'still'.

More Difficulty:
1. use swim fin.

HANGMAN'S KICK 3
Flexer
Holding
Benefits: arms, shoulders, side muscles, thigh, hips, waist, neck

With front to wall and hanging from side or ladder as in Hangman's Kick 1 and 2, keep legs together and toes pointed and swing whole of lower body to the right and left to maximum respective positions. Hold in the extreme positions as long as possible for good stretches, yet maintain good rhythm.

More Difficulty:
1. vigor, plus repetition;
2. do frontways first, then back-to-wall after;
3. in shallower water when facing wall so you have to bend knees to avoid touching bottom;
4. use swim fins.

DORSAL FLIP
Flexer
Floating
Benefits: small of back, shoulders, neck, stomach, thighs

Float leisurely on stomach maintaining float with small kicks and required movements of hands while arms extended out before you. Suddenly, throw head back as far as possible and raise both arms and thrust feet into air as far as capable. This will have effect of arching back. Hold for as long as possible. Then blow out air vigorously and let body flop back into water, yet keep starting position of float without great accentuation of movements of arms or feet. *Note*: This is an extremely difficult exercise with great benefit to small of back and stomach for a very small elevation of the arms and heels as you have to break the surface tension of the water through sheer muscle power, without leverage.

─── 63 ───

SOMERSAULTING
Flexer
Floating
Benefits: back, stomach, arms, lungs

Tread water, then tuck head downwards and pull upwards with arms. Keeping legs together and toes pointed, allow body to do full roll underwater. Come up for air when full circle completed. Repeat as required, holding breath as long as possible.

More Difficulty:
1. vigor;
2. do backward somersaults;
3. attempt two or three somersaults consecutively without breathing.

─── 64 ───

SUBMARINE 1
Flexer
Floating
Benefits: stomach, legs, side muscles

Kick off, raise one arm perpendicular above you and the other outstretched along the surface of the water while kicking a backstroke kick. Repeat with other arm raised and swap arms.

More Difficulty:
1. vigor of kick, plus distance;
2. use breaststroke-type kick;
3. use butterfly-type kick;
4. use swim fins to benefit thighs.

SUBMARINE 2
Flexer
Floating
Benefits: stomach, thighs, hips, hamstring, calf, foot and ankle

Treading water, then fling one leg out in front and other leg to the rear in a front-and-back scissors kick. Bring legs back together, then repeat scissors kick movement with other leg going to front and rear respectively. You will find you 'bob' up and down with each movement. Use this bobbing action to (a) get good movement of legs fore and aft and (b) vigor.

More Difficulty:
1. vigor to maintain stationary position;
2. stronger kicking forward concentrating on pointing toes to get front-of-thigh benefit;
3. use swim fins.

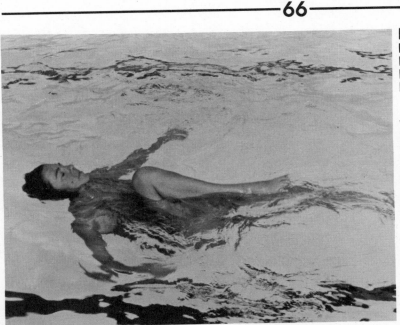

FLOATING TUCK 1
Flexer
Floating
Benefits: stomach, thighs, knees, buttocks, arms

Floating on back, supporting your float with small circular hand movements as vigorously as necessary to maintain float, bring one knee up to tuck as snugly into chest as possible, keeping the other leg straight and all toes pointed. Return to extended position and repeat with other leg.

More Difficulty:
1. vigor, plus repetition;
2. while knee is in tuck position, increase strength of hand movement to propel yourself backwards and forwards and increase distance.

FLOATING TUCK 2
Flexer
Floating
Benefits: stomach, thighs, knees, buttocks, arms

   Perform previous exercise (Floating Tuck 1) but bring both knees up to chest together and hold for good stretch as long as possible. Arms have to compensate for loss of area on surface of water to maintain buoyancy. Lower legs and repeat.

More Difficulty:
1. vigor, plus repetition;
2. while legs tucked, try for distance both backwards and forwards by use of stronger arm pulls through water.

BICYCLE
Flexer
Floating
Benefits: stomach, legs, back, hips, buttocks, feet and ankles

   Floating on back with float supported by hand paddling movements at side, kick vigorously as though pedalling a bicycle while maintaining equilibrium. Keep toes pointed all the time.

More Difficulty:
1. vigor, plus repetition;
2. coordinate stronger arm movements with kicking to propel forwards and backwards.

REVERSE SCISSORS LIFT
Flexer
Floating/holding
Benefits: back, stomach, legs, groins, buttocks, shoulders

With back to wall and floating face upwards, hold on to side as best you can to maintain float. Stretch legs out together, then open them as wide as possible. Hold for good stretch, then heave to try to lift legs out of the water, taking weight on shoulders as necessary. Try to get heels as far out as possible. Lower legs back to water. Bring legs together. Then repeat scissors and lift movement. Do as continuous exercise.

More Difficulty:
1. vigor, plus repetition;
2. variation by turning feet inwards and trying to lift legs while they are like that; ditto for feet turned outwards.

SUSPENDED ARCH
Stretcher or Flexer
Floating
Benefits: small of back, stomach, chest, thighs

Tread water. Fling arms upwards and outwards, throw head back and arch back as much as possible. Hold as long as possible to maintain float. Relax and repeat.

More Difficulty:
1. repetition.

PENDULUM
Flexer
Floating
Benefits: general body
(especially stomach, arms,
back, groin)

Tread water. Pull back
vigorously with arms to pull legs
through beneath you to extend
out in front. Legs should have
swung through together with
toes pointed. You are now
floating on back. Pause. Then
push torso and arms forward
and heave lower body back
beneath you to rear position so
that you are now floating on your
stomach. Legs should have
swung through open and in arcs
and have come together at top
of movement. Arms have
remained outstretched. Arch
back and hold this position for
good stretch of back and thighs.
Then duck head and vigorously
pull backwards with arms
swinging your body back
beneath to the legs-forward
position (legs together, toes
pointing again). You are now on
your back again.
Repeat these swings back and
forward.

More Difficulty:
1. vigor, plus repetition.

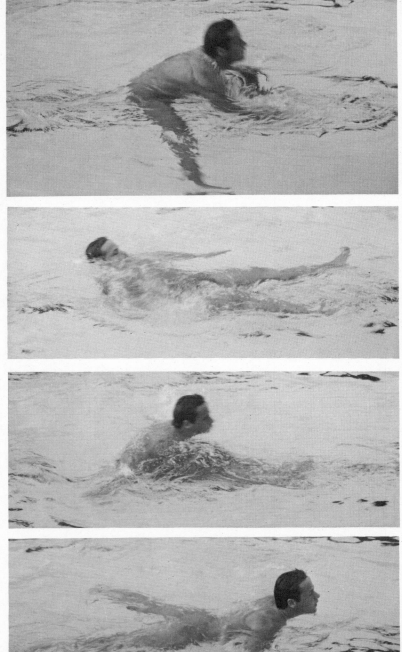

RUNNING
Flexer
Standing
Benefits: general body (especially legs, buttocks, ankles, chest)

Run up and down your pool. Hold your arms in a bent position so they stay above surface of water. Adjust the length of your strides according to the depth of the water. When running, surge with your left side with right leg; right side with left leg, etcetera.

More Difficulty:
1. vigor, plus distance;
2. deeper water (until mid-chest depth);
3. run backwards.

BALLET BAR
Stretcher
Standing
Benefits: groin, hamstring, calves, feet and ankles

In at least chest-depth, raise leg and put up on side keeping your other foot flat on bottom. Hold for initial groin and inner thigh stretch, then reach over to touch toes or, if possible, to reach beyond toes of raised leg Hold for good stretch.
Note: Leg heights of this nature are only for the really supple and/or superfit.

BODY BALL
Stretcher or Flexer
Floating
Benefits: back, spine, buttocks, thighs

Tread water, then vigorously bunch yourself into a ball by hugging knees to chest and tucking head in. Hold your arms around your knees hard, so that you are a 'tight' ball. Let yourself sink and keep tightness of grip until you bob back to the surface. Let go and return to treading water. Repeat frequently.

More Difficulty:
1. vigor, plus repetition.

FLOTSAM
Flexer
Floating
Benefits: arms, waist, back, buttocks, neck, hamstrings, lungs

Tread water, then vigorously double up to grab your calves as low as you can (hopefully around ankles). Keep legs straight and, even though sinking, pull head into your lap as far as possible by bending arms. Hold this position, keeping strain on parts of body affected until body bobs back to the surface. Release, breathe deeply, then repeat

WATER WALKING
Flexer
Floating
Benefits: stomach, legs, hips, waist, back, arms

Using hands as vigorous paddles and legs as 'thrashers', surge your body as high out of the water as possible and, endeavoring to maintain that height, 'walk' as far as you can. Relax to sink back to treading water. Then repeat.

More Difficulty:
1. vigor, plus distance;
2. try with legs motionless, taking all the strain on arms;
3. hold hands high in air and use legs as sole means of propulsion.

STAR FISH 1
Flexer
Floating
Benefits: stomach, side muscles, arms, groin, hips, back, legs

Treading water with arms stretched down your sides, suddenly heave arms upwards to horizontal stretch and, at same time, open legs to extreme scissors position. Repeat this as vigorously as you can, not minding that you will sink a little, then bob up to the surface. Be conscious of keeping your stomach in and chest out while doing routine to ensure good stretch during exercise.

More Difficulty:
1. vigor, plus repetition;
2. use hand paddles to increase strength required in arms.

STAR FISH 2
Flexer
Floating
Benefits: side muscles, arms, stomach, groin, legs

Float on back with arms extended and feet together. Take deep breath, pull arms through water to be in optimum open position while, at the same time, opening your legs to the extreme scissor position. Bring both arms and legs back to original position together. Breathe and repeat.

More Difficulty:
1. vigor, plus repetition;
2. use hand paddles to increase the strength you need.

WHIRLWINDING
Flexer
Floating
Benefits: general body (especially shoulders, upper arms, side muscles, thighs)

Instead of doing the backstroke, bring both arms out of the water at the same time and pull through the recovery stroke at the same time.

More Difficulty:
1. vigor, plus repetition;
2. use swim fins for greater leg development.
3. use hand paddles for greater shoulder and chest development.

PORPOISING 2
Flexer
Floating
Benefits: general body (especially back, calves, side muscles, lungs)

As with Porpoising 1 (Exercise 50), where you dive forwards in an arc to touch bottom then spring forward to break water further on before plunging back to bottom. But this time, turn 180 degrees so that you push off backwards. Do so vigorously. When in air above water, twist your body so that you plunge back into water face downwards again. You will have turned a full circle in the space of two dives.

More Difficulty:
1. repetition, plus distance.

ONE-LEGGED DOG PADDLE
Flexer
Floating
Benefits: general body (especially thighs, upper arms, side muscles, stomach)

Just before doing the dog paddle stroke, bend one knee up and grasp ankle. Keep this hold while dog paddling with other arm and leg. Change sides.

More Difficulty:
1. vigor, plus distance.

PRESS-UPS
Flexer
Standing/floating/holding
Benefits: upper arms, shoulders, chest, stomach, wrists

In at least waist-depth, place your hands flat on side about shoulder-width apart. Press up above side until arms are locked. Hold for good strain, then lower body as slowly as you can to starting position. Repeat as possible. Keep toes pointed and stomach in when in press. Also, try to avoid wriggling your body on the way up; go for clean and sharp movements upwards.

More Difficulty:
1. vigor, plus repetition;
2. longer hold in press position;
3. deeper water;
4. bend knees at right angles behind you and repeat exercise.

DEEP PRESS-UPS
Flexer
Floating/holding
Benefits: upper arms, shoulders, chest, stomach, wrists

In deep, hold on to side with hands at shoulder-width and let your body hang vertically in water with arms extended above you and your head below the surface. Then heave yourself up (giving sharp scissor kick if needed) to full press-up so that arms are locked in fully extended position below you. Hold as long as possible for good strain. Then slowly lower yourself to starting position. Repeat.

More Difficulty:
1. vigor, plus repetition;
2. when hanging, bend legs backwards. Keep them bent throughout exercise so that arms have to do more work.

BACK PRESS-UPS
Flexer
Standing/holding
Benefits: upper arms, shoulders, stomach, wrists, back

Repeat previous press-ups but do them with your back to the side of the pool. Repeat as possible.
Note: This exercise is better done at the corner of the pool where you can get a steadier purchase on two sides with your hands. Remember to keep hands no greater apart than your own back width to avoid slip in press-up position, which could do harm. Therefore, do not do this exercise too quickly – use repetition, not vigor.

11

Your Water Body: Beauty and Body Development

In this Section, we have broken down the exercises given in the previous two chapters into their 'body' constituent parts for you. The following categories will allow you to move along the beauty or body-development path you want to choose for yourself.

As I have already stressed earlier: water is an overall beneficial gym medium for you. Whenever you do any exercise in water, you are more likely to be giving benefit to another part of your body more than if you were doing the same exercise in a dryland gym, generally speaking. The more vigor and/or repetition, for example, you put into your water exercises, the wider the effect of the exercise is going to be on your body.

Thus, it is slightly more difficult to be precise when we are talking about which muscle or joint is going to get the most benefit from such-and-such an exercise; there might be a number of other muscles and/or joints benefiting just as much. (For example, we have already spoken about the exercising effect on the arms and hands when just keeping yourself afloat in some of the floating routines.)

You can develop your bust or firm up your buttocks, or go for the big bicep he-man look or just want that good swaying walk and good looks that come from the suppleness of being water fit.

Like everything else in the getting-fit realms of life, there is no magic formula to achieving that ideal-for-you look overnight.

You have to work at exercises fairly persistently to get yourself, say, a taut and terrific stomach. (There are also those boring other things called diets and good wholesome living!) If you want it, you'll persevere at the routines we give you in this book. If you don't, for heaven's sake, don't feel guilty about it. Just enjoy the water.

When you get more experienced in your pool gym, you will quickly learn which exercises are really specific for you and which are general-body ones. This is because water highlights our individuality in the way we move and so forth. You might exercise some part totally different than I do in the same exercise. You'll soon get to know which exercise does what to you. You'll soon be pulling them out of your repertoire at will when you want this-or-that benefit.

Not All Vanity

We don't have to use this Section all the time for our personal little (and absolutely justified!) vanities. We can use its cross-referencing facilities to help others – whether a child, or your expecting wife, or poor old sore Dad or Mum, or Granny.

Show them what exercises are best for them and then show them how to do them. Help them, support them. Introduce them to the specialised or generalised benefits you know they can get out of your pool gym.

Of course, it might be you who's got the muscle soreness or a bruised arm or somesuch or an ache in a joint. It might be yourself who's had a rotten day and needs to relax your neck and shoulder muscles because you know that goshdamn headache is just around the next tick of the clock.

Well, take yourself to your pool gym and ease into it. Then do the relaxation exercises you can select from this Section. It'll work and you'll feel good. It sure beats the heck out of popping painkillers and there's more room to move than in the bath. It's what philosophers and neurologists have been telling us all the time about water.

Arms and Shoulders

Upper Arms

Front Fanning ————————4————————

Fanning Beneath ————————5————————
   particular benefit when pulling
upwards

Fanning Vertically ————————6————————

Beacon 2 ————————9————————

Rainbow ————————10————————

Rainbow Circle ————————11————————

Arm Rounders ————————12————————

Side Roll ————————16————————

Half Press-Ups ————————17————————
   hold at press-in position longer

Back Swallow 1 ————————20————————

Shallow Boxing ————————22————————
   good during vigorous arm
recovery movement

Dog Paddling ————————27————————

Chest Puffing ————————28————————
   good when longer hold in
arched position, until nice strain

Water Disco 2 ————————31————————
   in More Difficulty phase

Kicking in Place 2 ————————34————————

Push and Pull ————————39————————

One-Arm Paddle ———————————41————————

Wall Shove ———————————42————————

Push, Pull and Shove ———————————43————————

Feet First ———————————52————————
    especially in More Difficulty
phase

Paddle Fanning ———————————53————————

Canoeing ———————————54————————

Hangman's Kick 1 ———————————59————————

Hangman's Kick 2 ———————————60————————

Hangman's Kick 3 ———————————61————————
    especially in More Difficulty
phase

Floating Tuck 1 ———————————66————————
    when going for pace and
distance

Floating Tuck 2 ———————————67————————
    when going for pace and
distance

Bicycle ———————————68————————
    in More Difficulty phase

Pendulum ———————————71————————
    when pulling arms through

Flotsam ———————————75————————

Water Walking ———————————76————————

Star Fish 1 ———————————77————————
    in More Difficulty phase

Arms and Shoulders

Star Fish 2 ——————78——————
  in More Difficulty phase

Whirlwinding ——————79——————

Porpoising 2 ——————80——————

One-Legged Dog Paddle ——————81——————

Press-Ups ——————82——————

Deep Press-Ups ——————83——————

Back Press-Ups ——————84——————

Lower Arms

Exercise no.

Front Fanning ——————4——————

Fanning Beneath ——————5——————
  push down hard each time

Fanning Vertically ——————6——————

Beacon 2 ——————9——————

Rainbow ——————10——————

Rainbow Circle ——————11——————

Arm Rounders ——————12——————

Dog Paddling ——————27——————

Push and Pull ——————39——————

One-Arm Paddle ——————41——————
  particularly good with strength
  of grip of holding arm

Arms and Shoulders

Wall Shove
    really straighten arms in
extended position
———————42———————

Push, Pull and Shove
    keep arms very straight and
grip really strong
———————43———————

Feet First ———————52———————

Paddle Fanning ———————53———————

Canoeing ———————54———————

Hangman's Kick 1 ———————59———————

Hangman's Kick 2 ———————60———————

Hangman's Kick 3 ———————61———————

Floating Tuck 1 ———————66———————

Floating Tuck 2 ———————67———————

Bicycle
    in More Difficulty phase
———————68———————

Pendulum ———————71———————

Flotsam ———————75———————

Water Walking ———————76———————

Star Fish 1 ———————77———————

Star Fish 2 ———————78———————

Whirlwinding ———————79———————

Porpoising 2 ———————80———————

One-Legged Dog Paddle ———————81———————

Arms and Shoulders

Press-Ups
    particularly initial heave to get above wall
————————82————————

Deep Press-Ups
    initial movement crucial on forearms
————————83————————

Back Press-Ups
    especially maintaining balance with good grip
————————84————————

Shoulders

Exercise no.

Front Fanning ————————4————————

Fanning Beneath ————————5————————

Fanning Vertically ————————6————————

Fan and Heave ————————7————————

Arm Rounders ————————12————————

Shallow Boxing
    especially in More Difficulty phase
————————22————————

Water Squats 2
    hold squat to take weight on arms
————————26————————

Dog Paddling ————————27————————

Water Disco 1 ————————30————————

Water Disco 2 ————————31————————

Kicking in Place 1 ————————33————————

Back Tuck ————————36————————

Arms and Shoulders

Back Scissors with Tuck ——————37——————

Jack Knife ——————38——————

Reverse Scissors ——————40——————

One-Arm Paddle ——————41——————

Push, Pull and Shove ——————43——————

Ship's Roll ——————44——————

Porpoising 1 ——————50——————

Squat Jumps ——————51——————

Feet First Sculling ——————52——————

Paddle Fanning ——————53——————

Canoeing ——————54——————

Back Swallow 2 ——————56——————

Sprint ——————58——————
'hunching' effect

Hangman's Kick 1 ——————59——————

Hangman's Kick 2 ——————60——————

Hangman's Kick 3 ——————61——————

Dorsal Flip ——————62——————

Submarine 1 ——————64——————

Reverse Scissors Lift ——————69——————

Pendulum ——————71——————

Arms and Shoulders

Star Fish 1 ————————77————————

Star Fish 2 ————————78————————

Whirlwinding ————————79————————
   especially in More Difficulty phase

Press-ups ————————82————————

Deep Press-Ups ————————83————————

Back Press-Ups ————————84————————

Wrists and hands

Note: Whenever you need propulsion or support from your arms and hands in any exercise, remember to turn the palms of your hands towards the direction your arms are moving, so that your hands form oars or 'cup' the water as they go.

If you remember to do this, you will not only get greater benefits from the exercises themselves, but will provide good general benefits for your wrists and hands.

If you particularly wish, say, to get your wrists stronger, you should concentrate on your palms pulling through the water whenever you're doing an exercise.

Some of the exercises given here, then, are those additional ones which put some part of your weight on to your wrists and hands. You may or may not want this.

Exercise no:

Calf Stretch ————————2————————

Half Press-Ups ————————17————————

Back Swallow 1 ————————20————————
   for hands; keep good grip

Kicking in Place 1 ————————33————————
   keeping good grip

One-Arm Paddle ————————41————————
   strength of grip

Wall Shove ————————42————————
   for grip

Push, Pull and Shove ————————43————————

Sprint ————————58————————
   bunching of fist effect

Press-Ups ————————82————————

Deep Press-Ups ————————83————————

Back Press-Ups ————————84————————

Back

Spine

	Exercise no.
Dog Paddling	27
Kicking in Place 1 especially butterfly kick	33
Back Tuck	36
Push and Pull	39
Back Swallow 2	56
Hangman's Kick 1	59
Hangman's Kick 2	60
Hangman's Kick 3	61
Somersaulting	63
Suspended Arch	70
Body Ball	74
Porpoising 2	80
Press-Ups	82
Deep Press-Ups	83
Back Press-Ups	84

Back Muscles

Exercise no.

Calf Stretch
pronounce arching of back on recovery movement ——————— 2 ———————

Fanning Beneath
arch back on upward stroke ——————— 5 ———————

Rainbow Circle
back straight in recovery ——————— 11 ———————

Back Swallow 1 ——————— 20 ———————

Sideswiping 1
when leg in back position, arch back and hold ——————— 23 ———————

Ballet Stretch ——————— 24 ———————

Dog Paddling ——————— 27 ———————

Chest Puffing ——————— 28 ———————

Water Disco 1 ——————— 30 ———————

Water Disco 2 ——————— 31 ———————

Corkscrew ——————— 32 ———————

Back Tuck ——————— 36 ———————

Back Scissors with Tuck ——————— 37 ———————

Jack knife ——————— 38 ———————

Wall Shove
degree of back arch ——————— 42 ———————

Push, Pull and Shove
degree of back arch ——————— 43 ———————

Ship Roll ———————44—————————

Hopping on Spot ———————48—————————
  keep back straight

Porpoising 1 ———————50—————————

Paddle Fanning ———————53—————————

Back Swallow 2 ———————56—————————

Sideswiping 2 ———————57—————————
  arch back when leg in rear
position

Dorsal Flip ———————62—————————

Somersaulting ———————63—————————

Reverse Scissors Lift ———————69—————————

Suspended Arch ———————70—————————

Pendulum ———————71—————————
  arch back as much as
possible when extended face
down with arms out before you
and feet behind

Running ———————72—————————

Body Ball ———————74—————————

Flotsam ———————75—————————

Water Walking ———————76—————————

Star Fish 1 ———————77—————————

Whirlwinding ———————79—————————

Porpoising 2 ———————80—————————

Back

One-Legged Dog Paddle —————81—————

Press-Ups —————82—————

Deep Press-Ups —————83—————

Back Press-Ups —————84—————

Buttocks

Exercise no.

Dangle Kick —————14—————
   in More Difficulty phase

Buttock Roll —————15—————

Groin Flex 2 —————19—————

Sideswiping 1 —————23—————

Water Squats 1 —————25—————

Water Squats 2 —————26—————

Hurdling —————29—————
   knee as high and as wide an
arc as possible

Water Disco 1 —————30—————

Water Disco 2 —————31—————

Back Tuck —————36—————

Back Scissors with Tuck —————37—————

Jack Knife —————38—————
   hold in legs-up position longer

Reverse Scissors —————40—————

Ship Roll ——————44——————

Running on Spot ——————45——————

Astride Jumping ——————46——————

Hopping Mad 1 ——————47——————

Hopping Mad 2 ——————49——————

Squat Jumps· ——————51——————

Sideswiping 2 ——————57——————

Sprint ——————58——————
  tensing effect

Floating Tuck 1 ——————66——————

Floating Tuck 2 ——————67——————

Bicycle ——————68——————

Reverse Scissors Lift ——————69——————

Body Ball ——————74——————

Flotsam ——————75——————

Legs
Calves

Exercise no.

Calf Stretch ——————2——————

Dangle Rounders ——————13——————
keeping toes pointed all the time

Dangle Kick ——————14——————

Water Squats 1 ——————25——————

Water Squats 2 ——————26——————

Dog Paddling ——————27——————

Water Disco 1 ——————30——————

Water Disco 2 ——————31——————

Kicking in Place 1 ——————33——————
especially using swim fins

Wall Shove ——————42——————
force feet flat against wall

Push, Pull and Shove ——————43——————
force feet flat against wall

Running on Spot ——————45——————

Hopping Mad 1 ——————47——————

Hopping Mad 2 ——————49——————

Porpoising 1 ——————50——————

Squat Jumps ——————51——————

Legs

Sideswiping 2 ——————57——————

Sprint ——————58——————

Submarine 1 ——————64——————
especially in More Difficulty phase

Submarine 2 ——————65——————

Bicycle ——————68——————

Pendulum ——————71——————

Running ——————72——————

Ballet Bar ——————73——————

Whirlwinding ——————79——————

Porpoising 2 ——————80——————

One-legged Dog Paddle ——————81——————

Feet and Ankles

Exercise no.

Storch Stretch ——————3——————

Dangle Rounders ——————13——————

Dangle Kick ——————14——————

Buttock Roll ——————15——————

Side Roll ——————16——————

Sideswiping 1 ——————23——————

Dog Paddling ——————27——————

Legs

Water Disco 1	————30————
Water Disco 2	————31————
Corkscrew	————32————
Kicking in Place 1 especially using swim fins	————33————
Back Tuck	————36————
Back Scissors with Tuck	————37————
Wall Shove force feet against wall	————42————
Push, Pull and Shove force feet against wall	————43————
Ship Roll	————44————
Running on Spot	————45————
Hopping Mad 1	————47————
Hopping on Spot	————48————
Porpoising 1	————50————
Dangle Kick 2	————55————
Sideswiping 2	————57————
Sprint	————58————
Submarine 2	————65————
Reverse Scissors Lift in More Difficulty phase	————69————
Running	————72————

Legs

Ballet Bar	73
Whirlwinding	79

Groin

Exercise no.

Groin Flex 1	18
Groin Flex 2	19
Water Splits	21
Hurdling	29
Kicking in Place 1 especially breaststroke phase	33
Kicking in Place 2	34
Scissors	35
Back Scissors with Tuck	37
Reverse Scissors	40
Astride Jumping	46
Hangman's Kick 1	59
Hangman's Kick 2	60
Pendulum	71
Ballet Bar	73
Star Fish 1	77
Star Fish 2	78

Legs

Hips

Exercise no.

Dangle Rounders ———————13———————

Sideswiping 1 ———————23———————

Water Squats 1 ———————25———————

Water Squats 2 ———————26———————

Dog Paddling ———————27———————

Hurdling ———————29———————

Water Disco 1 ———————30———————

Water Disco 2 ———————31———————

Kicking in Place 1 ———————33———————

Kicking in Place 2 ———————34———————

Push, Pull and Shove ———————43———————

Running on Spot ———————45———————

Astride Jumping ———————46———————

Hopping on Spot ———————48———————

Porpoising 1 ———————50———————

Squat Jumps ———————51———————

Sideswiping 2 ———————57———————

Sprint ———————58———————

Hangman's Kick 1 ———————59———————

Legs

Hangman's Kick 2	60
Hangman's Kick 3	61
Submarine 2	65
Bicycle	68
Pendulum	71
Running	72
Water Walking	76
Whirlwinding	79
One-legged Dog Paddle	81

Hamstring

Exercise no.

Groin Flex 1 keep foot of straightened leg cocked	18
Groin Flex 2	19
Sideswiping 1	23
Ballet Stretch cock upper foot	24
Water Squats 1	25
Water Squats 2	26
Dog Paddling	27
Water Disco 2 height of legs	31

98

Legs

Kicking in Place 1	——————33——————	
Jack Knife	——————38——————	
Wall Shove	——————42——————	
Push, Pull and Shove	——————43——————	
Running on Spot	——————45——————	
Hopping Mad 2 high kicking out front	——————49——————	
Porpoising 1	——————50——————	
Sideswiping 2	——————57——————	
Sprint	——————58——————	
Submarine 1 especially in More Difficulty phases	——————64——————	
Submarine 2	——————65——————	
Bicycle	——————68——————	
Pendulum	——————71——————	
Running	——————72——————	
Ballet Bar	——————73——————	
Flotsam	——————75——————	
Water Walking	——————76——————	
Whirlwinding	——————79——————	
Porpoising 2	——————80——————	
One-Legged Dog Paddle	——————81——————	

Knees

Exercise no.

Beacon 1	8
knees are pivot points; don't bend	
Beacon 2	9
knees are pivot points; don't bend	
Dangle Kick	14
Water Splits	21
stretch extended leg	
Water Squats 1	25
Water Squats 2	26
Water Disco 1	30
Water Disco 2	31
Kicking in Place 1	33
Wall Shove	42
Push, Pull and Shove	43
Running on Spot	45
Hopping Mad 2	49
Porpoising 1	50
Canoeing	54
Dangle Kick 2	55
Sprint	58

Legs

Submarine 1	64	
Floating Tuck 1	66	
Floating Tuck 2	67	
Bicycle	68	
Running	72	
Water Walking	76	
Whirlwinding	79	
One-legged Dog Paddle	81	

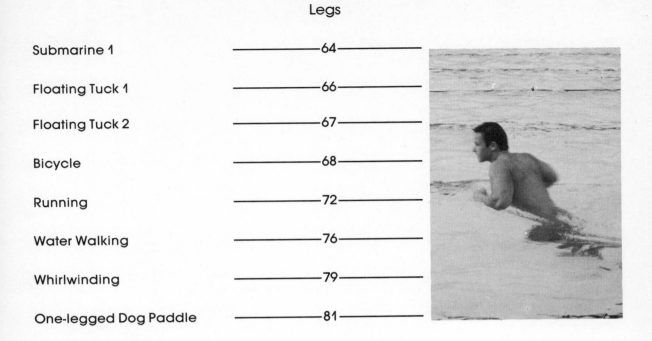

Thighs (front, rear, inner)

Exercise no.

Joy of Spring	1
Storch Stretch	3
Beacon 1 keep legs straight	8
Beacon 2 keep legs straight	9
Dangle Rounders	13
Dangle Kick	14
Groin Flex 1	18
Groin Flex 2	19
Sideswiping 1	23

Legs

Water Squats 1	25
Water Squats 2	26
Dog Paddling	27
Hurdling	29
Water Disco 1	30
Water Disco 2 height of legs·	31
Corkscrew	32
Kicking in Place 1	33
Scissors	35
Back Scissors with Tuck	37
Running on Spot	45
Astride Jumping	46
Hopping Mad 1	47
Hopping on spot	48
Hopping Mad 2	49
Porpoising 1	50
Squat Jumps	51
Canoeing	54
Dangle Kick 2	55
Sideswiping 2	57

Legs

Sprint	58
Hangman's Kick 1	59
Hangman's Kick 2	60
Hangman's Kick 3	61
Dorsal Flip	62
Submarine 2	65
Floating Tuck 1	66
Floating Tuck 2	67
Bicycle	68
Reverse Scissors Lift	69
Pendulum	71
Running	72
Water Walking	76
Star Fish 1	77
Star Fish 2	78
Whirlwinding	79
Porpoising 2	80
One-Legged Dog Paddle	81

Stomach and Chest
Abdomen

Exercise no.

Dangle Rounders —————13—————

Buttock Roll —————15—————

Chest Puffing —————28—————

Water Disco 1 —————30—————

Water Disco 2 —————31—————

Kicking in Place 1 —————33—————

Kicking in Place 2 —————34—————

Scissors —————35—————

Back Tuck —————36—————

Jack Knife —————38—————

Reverse Scissors —————40—————

One-Arm Paddle —————41—————

Push, Pull and Shove —————43—————

Hopping on Spot —————48—————
  concentrate on keeping
stomach muscles taut

Porpoising 1 —————50—————

Feet First Sculling —————52—————

Paddle Fanning —————53—————

Stomach and Chest

Dorsal Flip	62
Somersaulting	63
Submarine 1	64
Submarine 2	65
Floating Tuck 1	66
Floating Tuck 2	67
Bicycle	68
Reverse Scissors Lift	69
Suspended Arch	70
Pendulum	71
Running	72
Star Fish 1	77
Star Fish 2	78
Whirlwinding	79
Porpoising 2 especially with pronounced butterfly kick	80
One-Legged Dog Paddle	81
Press-Ups	82
Deep Press-Ups	83
Back Press-Ups	84

Chest (lungs)

Note: General swimming is great for your lungs, so try to do as many laps as you can. You don't have to be a top swimmer; just remember to breathe in really big and to expel *all* the air from your lungs each time, even if you're not about to break any record. If you're breathing out underwater, blow air out by making lots of bubbles; blow out healthily through both nose and mouth.

Exercise no.

Front Fanning	4
Fanning Beneath	5
Fanning Vertically	6
Fan and Heave expand chest for lungs	7
Arm Rounders expand chest for lungs	12
Chest Puffing	28
Porpoising 1	50
Squat Jumps especially in More Difficulty phase	51
Paddle Fanning	53
Back Swallow 2	56
Somersaulting	63
Suspended Arch	70
Pendulum	71
Running	72
Flotsam	75

Stomach and Chest

Whirlwinding —————79—————

Porpoising 2 —————80—————

One-Legged Dog Paddle —————81—————

Press-Ups —————82— —————

Deep Press-Ups —————83—————

Back Press-Ups —————84—————

Side Muscles (laterals)

Exercise no.

Fanning Vertically —————6—————

Fan and Heave —————7—————

Beacon 1 —————8—————

Beacon 2 —————9—————

Rainbow —————10—————

Rainbow Circle —————11—————

Side Roll —————16—————

Groin Flex 2 —————19—————

Ballet Stretch —————24—————

Dog Paddling —————27—————

Water Disco 1 —————30—————

Water Disco 2 —————31—————

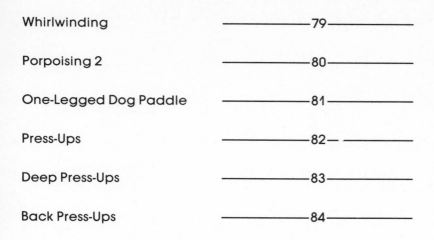

Stomach and Chest

Kicking in Place 1 ——————33——————

Scissors ——————35——————

Push and Pull ——————39——————

One-Arm Paddle ——————41——————

Push, Pull and Shove ——————43——————

Porpoising 1 ——————50——————

Canoeing ——————54——————

Hangman's Kick 1 ——————59——————

Hangman's Kick 2 ——————60——————

Hangman's Kick 3 ——————61——————

Submarine 1 ——————64——————

Running ——————72——————

Star Fish 1 ——————77——————

Star Fish 2 ——————78——————

Whirlwinding ——————79——————

Porpoising 2 ——————80——————

One-Legged Dog Paddle ——————81——————

Press-Ups ——————82——————

Deep Press-Ups ——————83——————

Back Press-Ups ——————84——————

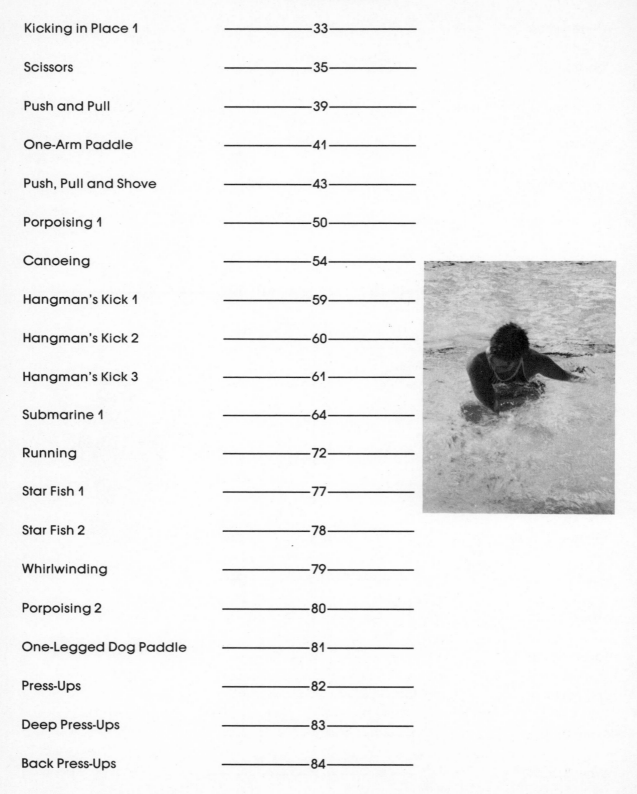

Waist

Exercise no.

Beacon 1	8
Beacon 2	9
Rainbow	10
Rainbow Circle	11
Shallow Boxing concentrate on swaying on hips	22
Water Disco 1	30
Water Disco 2	31
Ship Roll	44
Canoeing	54
Hangman's Kick 1	59
Hangman's Kick 2	60
Hangman's Kick 3	61
Pendulum	71
Running surging with torso from side-to-side	72
Water Walking	76

Neck

Note: General swimming and general play-around in water are good all-round activities for the neck. The following exercises are just the ones that assist your neck a little more.

Exercise no.

Rainbow Circle	11
pronounced head lean	
Back Swallow 1	20
Push and Pull	39
Porpoising 1	50
Back Swallow 2	56
Hangman's Kick 2	60
Dorsal Flip	62
Pendulum	71
Flotsam	75
Whirlwinding	79
Porpoising 2	80
One-Legged Dog Paddle	81

12
For Couples

The hook lines in a not-too-old Diana Ross song go:
'Upside down, boy, you're turning me
Inside out and round and round'
and as amazing as it sounds, it is almost a possible thing to happen if you exercise with another person in your pool gym.

Since the kindness of water makes us all Supermen and Superwomen, it lets us toss one another around in a way that we normal mortals could only dream about on dry land. What's more, we can echo the water by doing it kindly to the other person, in that, even if we are throwing them around, they're not really going to be hurt. That in itself gives a marvellous feeling of exhilaration.

Exercising together is strongly recommended. That's not just for the pleasure in it, either. Being able to take advantage of the buoyancy of water and therefore the 'lightness' of the heaviest of us, we can help our water mates achieve the maximum stretch and flexibility of movement of their muscles and limbs that only water can give. You can give support, lend balance, help to keep flotation, provide counter-weighting. In short, you can act just as though you are a marvellously adaptable piece of apparatus that, in a dryland gym, money just couldn't buy.

As equally to the point, your pool mate can be a marvellously adaptable piece of apparatus that money just couldn't buy for you!

Together, you can do exercises and routines that you could only dream about on dry land, or would be foolhardy to even try to execute on dry land. Imagine, on dry land, any but the most advanced athletes locking extended arms back-to-back and taking it in turns to rack the other person across their back! It might be a superb, advanced back stretcher, but it is also highly dangerous. In water, providing you do it in at least chest-high water to start with, it's a giggle.

Water exercises for couples combine fun with great fitness benefit. They can also be a way in which you can really help (at last!) someone dear to you to be able to do something positive against their injury or infirmity or arthritis or the like.

You can be in that pool gym beside them – helping them, guiding them, imparting confidence and great body benefit to them. You are giving them the confidence of fighting against what might be ailing them, whether it's just old age or a crippling condition under which you know they are losing their self-esteem.

Twosome water exercising is a form of serious play. Only the most lugubrious professional physiotherapist will not be giggling at the end of a twosome session. That's in the nature of water and in the nature of the good you are feeling it is doing you.

Naturally, care should be taken that you don't over-extend or use a limb that is tender or weak. But that is a matter of commonsense between you both. Don't be afraid to try, though.

Try all the exercises given here if you wish. Try the ones you think would be fun because you've just invented them. The only thing to do by way of caution is to start out carefully with each exercise and see how it works.

Generally, if you start out in chest-depth, you'll be able to carry, heave, stretch, yank, push'n'pull each other to your bodies' content without any problem. When you get more confident, go more shallow.

It's all a matter of experimentation. Remember that other song: *'He ain't heavy; he's my brother'*.

SWIMMING IN PLACE
Benefits: general body

Swimming in place with your feet hooked under the rail of your pool or somesuch is a good exercise, especially where the pool is not very large for laps. However, this is often most uncomfortable on your feet; if you get your pool mate to hold your ankles – or, indeed stand between your legs and hold you at the knees for greater support – you will find a great exercising bonus.

While being held, try:
1. freestyle stroke, breathing on either side;
2. breaststroke;
3. butterfly;
4. backstroke by turning over and floating supported face upwards.

FANNING TWOSOME
Benefits: side muscles, shoulders, stomach

Being held by the ankles or up to the knees by your pool mate, do Fanning exercises (Exercises 4, 5, 6) by:
1. while on back, pull arms through water from extended above head position through horizontal arc to at-your-sides position, and vice versa;
2. while face downwards, pull arms from being extended directly below you to widest open-arms position, trying to touch shoulder blades.

More Difficulty:
1. use hand paddles.

TOUCH TOES
Benefits: back, stomach, hamstrings, thighs

Being held from side under small of back face upwards, heave your torso out of the water and try to touch your toes. Your pool mate should not try to 'carry' you, just give you levering support.

PIGGYBACKS
Benefits: legs, stomach, back, shoulders

Carrying your pool mate on your back:
1. walk briskly through water;
2. run through water.
Though you'll be giggling quite a bit, try to be serious and to keep your torso facing straight ahead. Don't try to over-stride or you'll both topple and you won't be able to get up for giggling. Be serious!

JACK KNIFE
Benefits: back, neck, back of thighs, stomach

Being supported under your midrif but from the side, arch you back as much as you can by throwing your head back and trying to lift your feet free of the water. Repeat as continuous routine.

KICKING IN PLACE
Benefits: legs, stomach, back

Being held under the armpits, do:
1. freestyle kicking;
2. butterfly kicking;
3. breaststroke kicking;
4. backstroke kicking.
Concentrate on keeping feet mostly below surface of water to give best resistance to and benefits for thighs, etc.

More Difficulty:
1. use swim fins.

THE SUPPLERS
Benefits: back and stomach, and lower body generally

While being held under the armpits, and either on your back or on your stomach, do:
1. knee tucks by bringing both knees together up to tuck into your chest; lower them slowly as possible, and repeat;
2. repeated scissors opening and closing of straight legs;
3. combination routine of knees tuck and leg scissors (1 and 2 above);
4. kicking in a circular motion as though riding a bicycle;
5. making a straight periscope of one leg after the other by raising legs vertically, keeping knees straight and toes pointed;
6. full jack knives by bringing both straight legs over to try to touch your own head.

Repeat all above to make rhythm exercises of them.

LOUNGE KICKING
Benefits: back, thighs, calves, groin, stomach, feet and ankles

While being held under the armpits and floating on your side, do:
1. freestyle kicking, keeping legs as parallel to surface of water as possible. Since lower leg will meet more resistance, change over sides to get equal benefit;
2. butterly kicking;
3. raise top leg as high as possible, hold for good groin stretch, lower and repeat as routine. Change sides.

DRAGGING
Benefits: general body

Run or walk as hard as you can through the water while your pool mate hangs on to your waist and floats behind you as a 'drag'. Compete with each other on the number of times and speed of crossing the pool. Your pool mate should kick slightly to keep afloat.

DEAD WEIGHT
Benefits: (if you're above) arms, hamstrings, buttocks, stomach, shoulders; (if you're below) good stretching of arms, shoulders and side muscles

Stand on the side of the pool holding your pool mate by the wrists. He or she is in the pool, either in deep or (if pool is not deep enough) with knees bent so as not to be touching the bottom at the fully extended position. Keeping your legs straight, use your arm and shoulder muscles to raise and lower your pool mate successively. The water will give good assistance, but try to raise other person as high out of the water as possible when repeating exercise.
Make sure you lower the other person carefully. Do not jerk any movement that might cause damage to the shoulders.

JACKBOOT ASSIST
Benefits: hamstring, feet and ankle, back

While being held under the armpits and on your back, raise a stiff leg out of the water to as far as possible when keeping the other leg straight. When at the extreme elevated position, take hold of the knee with both hands and hold for a good stretch. Also try to lower leg but resist with hands. Hold again. Change legs.

THIGH STRETCH
Benefits: front thigh, back, stomach, neck

While being held under the armpits and floating face down, bend one knee and bring your foot up so that you can grasp it with your same-side hand. Pull in slowly for good stretch, concentrating on keeping the other leg straight. Release and let leg return to outstretch slowly. Repeat as necessary. Repeat with other leg.

JITTERBUG 1
Benefits: (if you're holding) arms, shoulders, stomach, back; (if you're being held) back, side muscles, shoulders

Stand in waist-depth with your pool mate's legs wrapped around your waist and his or her arms extended straight out beyond the head. Lock your own arms under the small of the other's back or buttocks. Pull upwards hard so that the other's small of the back is raised from the surface of the water. Then:
1. in raised position, swing your own body from as far left as possible to as far right as possible so that you are also dragging the other person to and fro across the surface; do as many times as possible, rest, then change direction;
2. both stretch backwards to create greater dragging effect through water.

JITTERBUG 2
Benefits: arms, shoulders, back, stomach, neck

Holding your pool mate by the wrists, your legs apart, and facing each other, so that his or her legs and part body are off the bottom between yours. Then push down with all your might and pull up with all your might to get the other person as far as possible in and out of the tunnel of your legs. Repeat as quick-succession routine.

COALMAN ULTRA-STRETCH

Benefits: (if you're doing the pulling) arms, side muscles, stomach, legs; (if you're being stretched) spine, stomach, side muscles, shoulders

Stand back-to-back in at least waist-deep water and hold hands above heads with good grips. Take in turns to bend forward and pull the other across your back as though you are a coalman and carrying a bag of coal on your back. Hold for mutual stretch and good strain. Release to repeat or to change roles.

More Difficulty:
1. this is easier in deeper water, harder in shallower water;
2. only with permission of the other, walk through water with load on your back.

SEE-SAW 1

Benefits: backs, legs, shoulders, stomachs

If the water, when you are sitting, does not come over shoulder level, sit facing each other at arm's-length distance, holding hands and with feet braced against each other's. Keeping strain on arms, rock back and forwards so that, one after the other, you throw your head back and arch your back as much as possible. Legs give leverage against each other. Get up beneficial mutual rhythm.

More Difficulty:
1. vigor, plus repetition.

SEE-SAW 2
Benefits: backs, legs, shoulders, stomachs

Instead of sitting, stand in at least waist-depth forming a V at your feet. Feet braced against each other and holding hands with arms at first braced in a cocked (or, say, forming 90 degrees at elbows) position. Take weight, then take it in turns to arch back and extend arms for good back stretch. The other partner gets benefit of holding on tight and supporting you. Repeat, then change roles.

More Difficulty:
1. vigor, plus repetition;
2. depth of water.

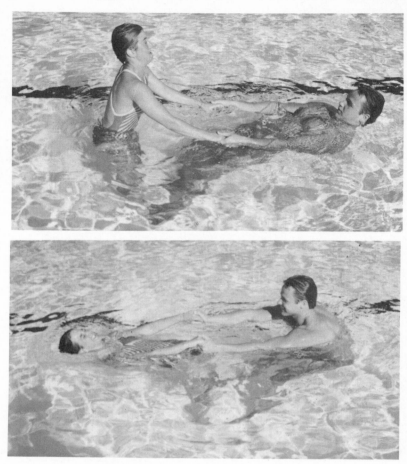

LOCOMOTIVE
Benefits: general body

Stand face-to-face in at least chest-depth and about half-arm length away. Grip hands by interlocking fingers only, one hand on top of the other. Both lean forward slightly and, one pushing while the other pulls, pump arms like opposite locomotive axles. Begin slowly and work up 'steam', getting faster and faster until one cries for mercy! Push and pull arms through to maximum positions.

More Difficulty:
1. vigor, plus repetition;
2. deeper water and moving against greater water resistance.

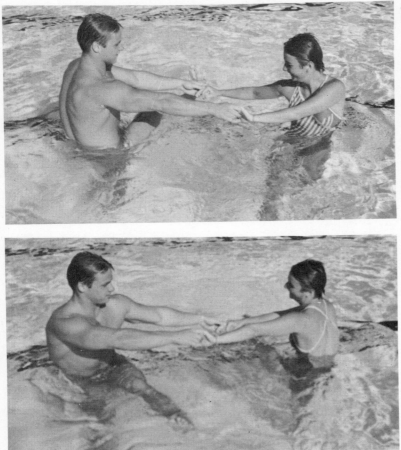

JIVING
Benefits: legs, waist, arms

Stand face-to-face in at least waist-depth and about half-arm length away from each other, lock hands and take mutual weight. Kick your right leg to the left at the same time as your pool mate kicks his or her right leg to the left. Kick your left leg to right at the same time as other does likewise. Repeat as though dancing, using your mutually strong grip to give leverage for a good 'jiving' bounce. Keep toes pointed.

More Difficulty:
1. vigor, plus repetition;
2. deeper water;
3. instead of kicking leg out, bring your knees up as high as practicable – right knees to the left, left knees to the right and so forth.

BOUNCING

Benefits: (on top) arms, chest, stomach; (on bottom) good side muscles, shoulder and stomach stretch

Stand face-to-face in at least mid-chest-depth, locking fingers or holding your pool mate by the wrists. If you are 'on bottom', you slowly let your body sink so that your pool mate gradually takes all your weight; you can do this in the shallow water by bending your knees behind you. Your partner braces against your weight, then proceeds to bounce you up and down in the water. Get your pool mate to lift you as high as possible keeping the back straight and chest out and stomach in. Repeat as necessary and change roles.

More Difficulty:
1. vigor, plus repetition;
2. height of repetitive lift;
3. depth of water.

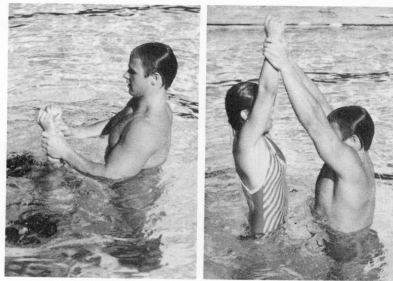

PYRAMID

Benefits: back, stomach, side muscles, groin, neck

In at least waist-depth, stand side by side holding hands at arm's length with other arms stretched out sideways. Pull against each other for good upper arm and inner legs stretch. Relax, then bring both outer arms across head in arcs to touch fingers in an apex of a pyramid above you. You are both leaning inwards giving your outer side and neck muscles a good stretch. Hold for benefits, then repeat.

13
Pregnancy

There was a time very recently when mothers-to-be were either medically advised – or believed that they had – to be careful of exercising. Nowadays, the advice is just to be wise about it.

The body goes through many changes in pregnancy, both externally and internally, but this is no reason to become overcautious about what you can do with it. Your body has a lot if inbuilt protection systems for both yourself and your child. So, after the usual and obligatory check with your doctor, you can with confidence exercise as much and as often and as varietally as you did before you fell into this wonderful state . . . except for that one change that makes it all a bit awkward – the sheer physical difficulty of coping with an enlarged midriff.

That's why you have to be more wise than careful. You have to adjust what you do in the form of exercising so that you do not exacerbate the existing physical discomfort to your bones, muscles and joints. If you're moderately healthy, that's all you really have to think about when exercising. Don't do anything you would not have done before you fell pregnant; but don't restrict yourself too much in what you used to do, either.

Floating within, floating without

In normal circumstances, there is no danger either to yourself, or baby, or for prematurity in good, vigorous exercising.

Whether you exercise extensively or not and whether you do this-or-that exercising or not, is again up to your own outlook and physical individuality. This is where water comes in so nicely for you. It is smooth and it's kind, and it gives you the pleasure of confidence to do exercises that might well be physically uncomfortable for you on dry land. While your baby floats within, you can float without.

Your doctor would have advised you how well nature has protected your baby in the womb, so you can water exercise with full confidence in the knowledge that you are not going to do something disastrous.

You merely have to follow the same old rules as you would apply to exercising before pregnancy. Start slowly; do the moderate stretching routines first; ensure you churn up the energy-carrying blood with good but gentle warm-ups, then do the flexer exercises as you physically or psychologically feel fit to do.

Your child is protected by the spine and the pelvis – together with the muscles and tissues that give swaddling to them and with that marvellous dampening, amniotic fluid – so you must think of your own body when exercising.

It is not the body you knew a few months ago. In straight physical terms alone, that wondrously enlarged 'front' that you are carrying – or will carry – has shifted your centre of gravity. Your back, your pelvis, your legs – in fact practically all of your bones, muscles and joints – have to adjust to that new physical condition. That's why and where you're getting some of those aches and pains. Hopefully, they are only minor discomforts.

This means that you must look to exercise those body parts that are most likely to be affected – the back, the pelvic region, the chest, the legs.

If you concentrate on exercising – let's call it relieving – these areas first, then you're brightening up your body to be a better, more adjusted 'edifice', as it were, to carry that extra weight in that upsetting-centre-of-gravity place. Those aches and pains and those cramps and those twinges of an unsupple muscle being in one unusual place too long will diminish a good deal; if not disappear altogether.

Since you are reading this book, you won't be surprised to hear that water is by far the best medium that you can exercise in. There's all the obvious reasons that we've discussed – the buoyancy, the 'soft' resistance and so forth. But these are even more heightened when you are pregnant.

You immerse yourself in your pool and you will almost certainly hear yourself sigh with relief when 'the weight' is lifted from you.

It's not only the weight, either. It's the freedom of movement suddenly possible. On dry land, it's much harder to swing your body around very easily when you're close to your time.

In water, though, it's all hunky-dory. I know you won't be surprised at the freedom and the sense of freedom that water brings to you, but I do hope you will be pleasantly surprised at the variety of exercise activities you can do in your pool gym. That belly is suddenly and blissfully not the same awkward protuberance.

Not All Beer and Skittles

Comfort during pregnancy is not, of course, the only reason why you should exercise, preferably in water.

There is going to come a time when that great moment arrives and you will realise how much fitness Nature demands of you at that time. Giving birth is a strenuous activity! Even when the birth goes swimmingly, if I can use that term, there will be enormous demands on your strength and endurance. Indeed, many superfit athletes would be absolutely amazed at the essential demands put on the body during the act of giving birth.

This is the part of pregnancy in which your exercising is not just for you, but also for your baby. Your child is not going to benefit too greatly by the exercises you're doing during those first nine months, but he or she is going to get incalculable benefits when your toned-up muscles and joints work superbly as and when and for as long as you both need it . . . and that, of course, is at the moment of birth.

Then there's the post-natal period. We all know that the major physical problem post-natally is the muscles not returning to their former glories. A muscle of good toning and strong suppleness due to good exercising (water, of course!) will have the essential restitution to recover from the trauma of birth-stretching and greater resilience to recover more quickly and more completely. Beyond the demands of childbirth, muscles have bodily duties, of course, so the better you contrive to improve their condition, the more assured you can be that you will recover completely. Take the muscles of the pelvic floor, for example. Without full recovery, so many of your bodily 'functions' wouldn't be restored fully.

Why Water, then?

Put simply, water allows you to exercise with great suppleness and greater energy at any time during pregnancy.

It's that buoyancy, yes. It's that softness, yes. It's also because with the greater freedom of movement, you simply do not get so fatigued when exercising.

And no matter what else is said, the greater the time, combined with the greater the suppleness possible, that is spent on toning yourself up will make the actual fact of the real thing less arduous.

There's also the psychological aspect of exercising with a sense of freedom you didn't think possible while being absolutely confident that you are not going to bring down some jarring (or so) harm to baby. You know, and we all keep telling you, that Nature has protected baby well enough anyway for that not to happen. But you wouldn't be human if there wasn't that little nagging doubt that the experts might be wrong . . . In water, you don't need that nagging doubt.

That One Last Benefit

That's confidence. You've got your body toned up; you're ready for the effort naturally needed on the big day; you're going to be able to recover so quickly that you'll be romping with your beautiful little child in as short a time as possible. You've got as much endurance, strength and resilience as you were hoping to get – and you got it in a painless pain-relieving, enjoyable way – in water. One of Nature's major elements – water – has communicated its pleasure with you and, while exercising in it, you have communicated your pleasure with it.

That's an advantage few can write about. It's the confidence of a sense of well-being.

Water exercise for it.

Breathing

You should know by now that you don't have to be able to swim to enjoy the benefits of water exercising. You also know that, rightly, great store is given to breathing techniques and routines to prepare you for childbirth.

Water is a great way to practise and develop your control of breathing, whether you are a swimmer or a non-swimmer.

If you're a swimmer, ensure that you concentrate on rhythmic underwater breathing even if you're doing a casual breaststroke lap or two. Ensure that you expel all the air from your lungs by really blowing those bubbles out into the water through both your nose and mouth, if you wish. With each breath, adjust your stroke timing so that you gulp in a whole lungful of air, such that you feel your chest expanding.

Even when you are doing your water exercises, keep at least half a mind on breathing strongly as the following advice indicates.

If you're a non-swimmer, try to get into the automatic routine of doing whatever exercises are possible with at least part of your mouth in the water when you are breathing out. Try to concentrate on breathing out lots of bubbles. It will give you a physical sign that you are really breathing out strongly and evenly. Naturally, if you do this, you're going to breathe in pretty strongly, too! But, in this phase, keep that half a mind on ensuring that you do so as strongly and evenly as you breathed out.

Swimmer or non-swimmer, please remember to adapt the rhythm and vigor of your exercises to the breathing aspect. The one will follow the other after a while, so that your breathing will automatically get quicker (yet still controlled) the more vigorously you exercise, but keep your breathing well in mind until you are doing it automatically.

The Pelvic Muscles

You don't need to have described the muscles that run like a truss under your torso and between your legs. You can feel them when you are on the toilet stopping your voiding motions. You can also feel them very pleasurably when you are making love.

In your condition, you'll realise how important this muscular region is for you. It is literally the major muscular sling that is supporting the extra wombic load you are carrying. Yet it also has to cope with the proper functioning of your bladder and so forth at the same time.

It's a muscle region that you must keep toned up with exercising, especially during pregnancy. We all should keep it toned up all through our lives, whether we're female or male, but pregnancy is that special time for this. The proper functioning of those lower outlets and inlets of your body during and (probably even more importantly) after pregnancy is absolutely imperative for your self-esteem.

The nice thing about this imperativeness is that the pelvic muscle is so easy to exercise. You only have to keep making the muscular movement of, say, shutting off your urine flow or stopping rectal void or squeezing your vaginal walls, and you're exercising the right way.

The trick during pregnancy is to remember to do these squeezing movements even more than usual.

So, when you're water exercising, remember to try to tighten and relax, tighten and relax these muscles whenever possible. If possible, this should be with every exercise. Like breathing, this should be a matter of water-exercising habit.

Be Your Own Exercise Supervisor

Just as you were your own coach when you were water exercising before the happy event came, so you should set your own exercise routine while you are pregnant.

The aim is still the same: To keep toning, and to keep your body in preparation for what lies ahead, exercise regularly – for half an hour or so. But do so by setting your own routine.

You are not an Average Type, and your daily physical and mental condition changes in accordance with the special you, not with some standard chart.

There is nothing inherently wrong with standard charts, except where they become counter-productive if they are starting to make you feel you're letting some mythical side down each day by not feeling like performing as you 'should'.

Forget that. Your child's not going to suffer.

Some days, you might just want to jump into your pool gym and whoopee around. Good; it's all exercise.

Again, if you like the exercise routine and don't want to keep varying what exercises you do, okay. Why not? Just try to get a trend over days or weeks of some improvement in vigor, length of time, or (with the same vigor and length of time) less strenuousness.

The Exercise Suggestions

We use the term 'Suggestions' here because, in water, you could really choose any of the exercises we've given in the earlier chapters, bar some like a few of the twosome ones.

However, as I have said, you have to be wise about exercising now that you have that 'added' responsibility.

What we would like to do, then, is to offer you a general approach that should be good for most people, followed by a series of basic exercises that either could be a good enough group in its own right, or should comprise good lead-through routines during the initial moments of your exercising.

Remember, you don't have to be a swimmer at all to exercise in water or to follow these suggestions.

Exercise Preparation

It is always advisable to get yourself in a relaxed frame of mind and body before you begin.

You can follow one of your own tried-and-proven techniques of relaxing on dry land, if you wish. If you haven't got a tried-and-proven technique, then the simplest way is to lie down on something comfortable, where it's quiet and familiar. Depending on how far you're 'gone', you might want to use pillows under your neck and shoulders and perhaps under your knees. Just lie there; unhurriedly push intruding thoughts aside; think of a number or a name that has, say, two syllables and repeat it lullingly and silently to yourself over and over again. When this 'name' is logged in your mind, keep repeating it with half a mind and, with the other half, concentrate on your toes to relax them, then on your feet to relax them, and so on as you mentally work your way up your body.

if you don't want to do this on dry land, float. Yes, float. It really is a most natural way of relaxing. Indeed, if you don't relax, you're going to find it very difficult to float!

I suggest you first jump around in the water a little bit to get warmer than you might be, but then quickly get down to floating. I guarantee that each time you do it you will feel the immense relief of that charming bundle of 'weight' being lifted from you. You'll get that exhilaration of not being awkward, in a sense, again.

If you're a swimmer, you'll be able to float even in very shallow water. That's all that's needed.

If you're a non-swimmer, simply hold on to the pool ladder or the side of the pool or rest your shoulders on the steps and let your legs float away from you. You'll be face up, of course! Depending on how accustomed you are at it, you might need to kick a little to get your feet to the surface and keep them there, but you should be able to do it with the smallest of kicks.

One trick is to fill your lungs with air, throw your head right back and puff your chest right out. Breathe very shallowly and smoothly after that and you'll soon learn the floating trick.

You'll know when to stop the floating/relaxing part, because you'll simply feel that's enough for the time being and you're keen to engage in another activity.

The Exercises

Most pregnancy-fitness programs generally concentrate on the regions of the spine, pelvis and abdomen . . . and that's right, given the particular process of childbirth you're about to go through.

Another advantage of exercising in water, though, is that you'll generally exercise more muscles or joints or whathaveyou for any one other given exercise. This is because water 'bathes' you in resistance.

Try to start with the exercises given here in this chapter and progress as you wish, and how you wish, to the other exercises in Chapters 9, 10, 11 and 12.

Water exercises will supplement those great benefits you're already getting if you're a swimmer, so do your laps as before.

However, swimmer or non-swimmer, always try to remember the two basic approaches to each and every exercise: The first is strong, controlled and regular breathing. The second is squeezing and relaxing the muscles of the pelvic base.

Remember: Get a breathing pattern. Exhale on action phase. Inhale on relaxation phase.

The Post-natal Period

Your medical advisor will be guiding you as to approved exercises immediately after childbirth, especially in the first few days when you are more than likely to be still bed-bound. Depending on the experience you have had, these exercises will be gentle feet, legs, back, waist, arms and neck flexers and stretchers, either when lying in the bed itself or sitting in a chair.

It will be when you are given the green light to begin full recuperative exercising that you will want to choose those exercises for you from Chapter 11. This will usually be after a month or so, but that will depend on your individual condition, fitness, state of recovery, and so forth. As you grow in confidence and competence, certainly the abdominal routines listed in Chapter 11 will feature prominently in your program.

As before, you should learn to listen to your body and be your own coach with regards to what you think is necessary for you to continue on a getting-better-every-day fitness course.

The two things you remembered while you were exercising pre-natally are just as important now – breathing and exercising the muscles around the perineum. With breathing, remember to 'Get a breathing pattern. Exhale on action phase. Inhale on relaxation phase'. Whenever you are contracting the abdomen, remember to really blow out. With the muscles of the pelvic floor, remember to tighten and relax them as much and as often as you can throughout each and every day.

You and Your Baby in Water

You don't need to wait until that month or more to get back into the pool, however. As soon as you are up and about, why don't you take your child into the pool with you? There you can relax with him or her, or glide around slowly. It's much the same as your last few days of pregnancy, but this time your baby will be in your arms rather than in your womb.

The water *must* be warm; and you *must* take great care in getting in or out of the water, even if, as we recommend, someone is helping you.

The joy of the first few post-natal days is sharing the experience of the world with your baby. That joy – and the bond that comes from it – will be given greater intimacy when you begin to share the soft experience of water. You will be amazed how relaxed the new-born child is in warm water and how immediately the bond between you seems to take on a new dimension.

Since the infant has been floating in your womb all those months, you are really extending a water experience together in a different way and medium. This time, your child is in your arms and this time your child is sensing the safety of your confidence and love.

Note: You can use these exercises as the basis of your exercising or your whole exercise program. Alternatively, you might be water- and pregnancy-confident enough to choose your own exercises by looking up Chapters 9, 10 and/or 11.

SPINE STRETCH
Stretcher
Standing/holding
Benefits: spine, lower back muscles, side muscles, buttocks

Stand a couple of feet away from the side wall with feet slightly apart. Take a good grip of the side while standing reasonably upright. Push your bottom out and lower your head, taking the strain on your arms. Hold for a good stretch along your spine.

SCISSORS
Stretcher/Flexer
Holding
Benefits: inner thighs, buttocks, abdomen, hips

In waist-deep water, spread your arms out along the side with your back to the wall so that you are reasonably supporting yourself. *If need be, you can keep your heels on the bottom throughout the exercise.* Let your legs float up as much as is easily done, then open and close your legs either for good stretching of the groin, or as a rhythmic exercise. Keep your toes pointed.

HALF JACK KNIFE
Flexer
Holding
Benefits: abdomen, buttocks, back muscles, front thighs, hips

As in Exercise 107, with back to wall and arms spread out along side in weight support, bring legs together and lift to try to break water surface with your toes. Lower legs and repeat. Keep toes pointed at all times.
Note: as with previous exercise, you may rest your heels on the bottom as necessary.
Repeat as:
1. one leg at a time with other leg bent.

TUCK
Flexer
Holding
Benefits: abdomen, buttocks, side muscles, hips

In similar position, bring knees up together in bent position to tuck up against your belly. Lower legs to be straight out before you. Repeat as rhythm exercise. Keep toes pointed. Heels may rest on bottom in stationary position.

HIPS TWIST
Stretcher/Flexer
Holding
Benefits: abdomen, waist, side muscles

In similar position, with back to wall and arms spread along side wall in weight support, twist your body from the waist down in one direction after the other. *Note*: as previously, heels may rest on bottom as necessary. Do this exercise with the following variations;

1. both legs stretched out together with toes pointing, then twist both, keeping your legs straight and heels together. Keep your torso facing straight ahead as much as possible.
2. bend legs into the tuck position and repeat, twist to and fro while keeping them there.

BACK PUSH
Stretcher/Flexer
Standing/holding
Benefits: back, back of thighs

In appropriate depth, so that you can have your arms spread out along the sides and stand comfortably on bottom in a knees-bent position. Push stomach forward and arch your back as much as is comfortable. Hold for good stretch or repeat as a rhythmic exercise.

SIDE KICK
Flexer
Holding
Benefits: waist, hips, groin, inner thigh

With back to the wall and arms spread out along the side in weight support, move right leg out to the right as far as it will go while keeping your torso facing the front. Hold for a short time, then move left leg over to join right leg until your heels are together again. Hold. Bring both legs back to front. Then repeat with left leg going to the left, and right leg following after. Keep toes pointed all the time. *Note*: heels can scrape along the bottom if need be.

ARMS FANNING
Flexer
Standing or kneeling
Benefits: waist, abdomen, upper arms, hips

In up to shoulder-depth, stand or kneel in water and, turning your palms each time to cup the water in the same directions as your arms are moving:
1. extend arms straight in front of you, back of hands touching; pull arms through to widest possible open-arm position; pull arms back through water to starting position.
2. repeat 1 above, but start with hands down by side and fan arms vertically up to surface of water and back again.
3. starting with hands crossed in front of you when arms extended straight down, fan your arms around your body as though outlining the hem of a skirt; bring back to your front and repeat.

WATER BALLET SQUATS
Stretcher/Flexer
Standing and/or holding
Benefits: inner thigh, groin, back, abdomen

Standing in mid-belly-depth and facing and holding on to side. Keep your back straight and chest out at all times. Squat on haunches as much as possible by:
1. keeping toes pointing to front and bending knees frontwards;
2. standing with heels together and toes pointing outwards; bend with the knees pointing out sideways; hold in open-knee position for good stretch.

SPLITS
Stretcher
Standing/holding
Benefits: inner thighs, abdomen, upper arms

Stand facing the wall and hold on to it with both hands. Feet apart. Take the weight on your arms and extend your legs apart as far as you can. Gradually let some of the weight come back to your body. Hold for good stretch. Return to starting position and repeat as necessary.

Do exercise as variation on leaning to one side as far as possible to get good groin stretch. Keep outer leg straight as possible and transfer your weight to be above your bent knee. Repeat on other side.

KICKING
Flexer
Floating/holding
Benefits: legs, abdomen, feet and ankles, side muscles, hips

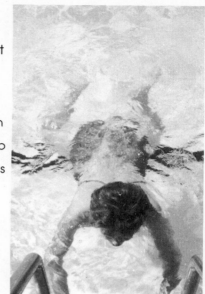

Hold on to side with arms outstretched while face downwards. Breathe regularly in and out of water if you're capable of doing so; if not, keep your head out of the water to breathe. Repeat the following as necessary:
1. freestyle kick;
2. butterfly kick;
3. breaststroke kick;
4. kick as though you are riding a bicycle.
Try not to break the surface of the water too much with your feet, but utilise benefits of the resistance of the water on your thighs, etcetera.

HORIZONTAL, FLOATING AND VERTICAL EXERCISES

These will move you into the areas of either being a swimmer or sufficiently confident and advanced in water exercising.

For the horizontal exercises, you will hold on to the side or the ladder of the pool and do your exercises either face down or face upwards.

For the floating exercises, you will have to be a swimmer.

For the vertical exercises, you will have to be confident of being in either water out of your depth or doing the routines with knees bent up beneath you. The latter, of course, is harder.

What all of these do is to bring the muscles of the torso and arms into play more, because it is the shoulders and the arms that often provide the necessary leverage needed for this-or-that exercise.

If your shoulder, arm, upper side and chest muscles are in fine fettle, it'll help you enormously when all that concentrated 'pushing' needs to be done – and done well.

So, adapt Exercises 106, 110, 111 and 115 of this chapter as necessary.

Also see the appropriate exercises in Chapters 9, 10, 11 and 12.

14
For Arthritis, Injuries, Joint Disorders

This chapter is for those who wish to help speed up their recovery, or having been unfortunate sufferers of one or other of these infirmities, wish to do as much as possible to prevent either a drastic remission or a reoccurrence. Water is a prime medium for the relief of conditions that are causing you pain or discomfort in your limbs, its 'softness' is almost a blessing for you. This is especially true in the initial recovery stages, when you know you have to keep yourself in as good trim as possible, yet dread the thought of exercising the part or parts of your body affected.

Water exercising is a good way to start out on your program of recovery – and one of the best means by which to carry on to full recovery. If nothing else, it helps to impart to you a quicker confidence to achieve good flexibility, then strength and endurance to your recuperating body. When, in those first few moments of initial flexing, you feel the natural response of water to softly resist you, you might feel, like many do, that somehow the discomfort doesn't feel as bad as on dry land. From there, confidence grows and, with it, so can the speed of your recovery, given the obvious condition that you're doing the right exercises for your particular complaint.

The increased flexibility that comes from water exercising permits greater ease and range of motion for ailing muscles. Improvement is not just from the exercise itself, but from the 'new' awareness you will get about how to move without pain against the gentle resistance of water. In water, it will seem much clearer to you which muscles or joints you are using, for that is in the nature of the higher perceptions about your environment that you get when immersed. You are able to focus the water itself, your exercise and your breathing on the area that is causing you pain or discomfort. This will tend to alleviate the problem more readily, if only because you learn and comprehend alternative ways of using your muscles to bypass the afflicted area.

Like everything, when you are trying to recover or to gain relief time, you must be cautious. You must take care not only that you are not being too eager to begin exercising (or not eager enough!), but also that you know what you are doing and should do.

Medical Advice

There are so many conditions of arthritis, injuries and joint disorders that it is impossible to give specific water-gym instructions to cover all early-recovery cases. There are general basic rules, of course. A joint, for example, needs to get careful initial manipulation in much the same way as if it was affected by arthritis or a sports injury or a car accident, and so forth.

However, as much as it is said so often, it is imperative that you consult your medical advisor before you begin any sort of exercise at all, let alone those exercises requiring vigor.

Your medical advisor will almost certainly talk to you about exercising and the way you should live and eat, yet you should not let it all stop there if that advice is only of a general nature. If you want to wisely exercise in water, then take this book along to him or her and point out those exercises you plan to do over a course of time. Get *specific* advice. You will either get better advice or, if he or she doesn't know if this-or-that exercise is good or bad for you, then you'll get advice on where to go to learn about it. Either way, you're ahead.

You are also going to get a lot more confident far more quickly if you know exactly what to do and how and when to do it.

Ask your family to help you out. If you've got difficulty moving, then they can find out for you. Get them to explain it to you. Get them to show you how to do this-or-that exercise. Get them in the water with you to hold you, steady you, help you gain in purpose and confidence. They'll love doing it because they can actually help you as they cannot do on dry land; they can lift you; they can support you more readily.

They will feel useful, and you won't feel so useless. That's water; the great equaliser.

Exercising

One of the basics I spoke about is this: you must avoid sudden movements of the injured or affected part of your body. You should never do this when you are starting out your exercise period even when you are fit all over. It can be absolutely counter-productive to jerk or overstretch an injured part. So make sure you prepare yourself for exercising first. Do the basic stretching exercises as given in Chapter 9, followed or preceded by careful warm-ups.

Try to get as much of the whole body warmed up and rearing to go before you concentrate on your maverick part.

Remember, too, that you've been ill and therefore have to build up your stamina in order to be able to exercise for recuperation. Don't forget the rest of your body; choose those exercises from Chapters 9 and 10 that you know are for you because you like them and can do them reasonably comfortably with the healthy parts of you.

More Than Confidence

Often we are more affected by illness or injury than we realise, because it is a mental strain as well. Sometimes we're not sleeping as well as we should be for good recovery because of the discomfort. Sometimes, it's the distress of feeling helpless or dependent upon others who you know you're inconveniencing. Often there are strangers around and you can't relax – or you're just mopey about the whole affair.

Take to the water, then. It will relax you far more than anything else. You can just literally 'drift around'. It will help you regain control of your mind and better your mind control. You will relax, often with a great load taken off both mind and body alike at the same time. But beware . . . there is one danger with this if you're ill or injured.

That is over-confidence.

Warning

I have heard more than once that people have felt so relaxed and confident in their water gym that they forgot the actual condition of their infirmity. They've forgotten how much early-days it is. They've actually over-moved or over-stretched a muscle or a joint or a ligament. The end result is that they have actually done themselves more damage than if they didn't exercise the part at all.

These are extremely rare incidents, but please remember to take it carefully at first. Don't get over-confident too quickly, just because you have found water a wonderful freedom-giver all of a sudden. Unfortunately, there is no miraculous alternative to the necessity of you 'proceeding with slow haste'.

The Exercises

Stretch out and warm up first, always. That can be warm up then stretch out, if you psychologically prefer. Only after you have done these and have started most slowly and carefully should you go into your specific recuperating exercises.

The Exercises For You

Your medical advisor should have discussed with you these recuperating exercises one by one. If need be, you will be getting one of your loved ones either to actively help you or to watch over you in supervision, particularly in the initial stages of your exercising.

In addition, Chapter 11 will suggest to you which routines will add variety to your self-imposed program in order to regain some, if not all, of that former suppleness and strength in your affected part. Again, use experimentation cautiously until you are well progressed.

Feet and Ankles - and Hands and Wrists

These are often the major areas of general and sport injuries, as well as arthritis problem areas.

In your water gym, you will find exercises which have specific benefits to these areas.

However, a great many of the exercises can also be of continuous benefit to your feet and ankles if you remember to keep your toes pointed or your feet cocked.

Likewise with your hands and wrists. If you remember to use your hands as paddles, whereby you turn your palms towards the direction your arms are moving each time, then you will also gain continuous benefits to these areas.

Conversely, you should be careful to remember to go carefully with any water exercise that may have side effects if feet or ankles or hands or wrists are your problem areas.

The Basic Routines

Until you are reaching proficiency and specialisation, we strongly suggest that you assimilate the following basic exercises as the necessary part, if not the whole, of your water gym time: (*Eliminate the basic exercise or exercises that are likely to do hurt or damage to your affected part.*)

Exercise no.

Calf Stretch	2
Front Fanning	4
Fanning Vertically	6
Beacon 1	8
Rainbow	10
Dangle Kick	14
Half Press-Ups	17
Groin Flex 1	18
Back Swallow 1	20
Shallow Boxing	22
Sideswiping 1	23
Water Disco 1	30
Kicking in Place	33
Running on Spot	45
Spine Stretch	106
Scissors	107
Hips Twist	110

Arthritis Sufferers

If a joint is inflamed, rest and treatment are the only cures for it; exercise can only do it more harm – even water exercise! Keep any workload off it during any flare up. Wait until the attack has subsided before you recommence exercising it.

Hopefully, exercising in your water gym will bring your condition under control for much longer periods – and make the next attack, should it come, far less distressing for you. That sort of relief will not come overnight. If this is any longlasting counter to arthritic joints, then it's keeping them moving healthily over a full range of movements over a long period. It is therefore strongly recommended that you keep up a frequent habit of exercising, both specifically for the affected joint or joints and for your general wellbeing.

Since arthritis effectively materialises itself as a joint disorder, then exercising with the full extent of gravity on your troubled area can become an inflammable problem. That is one of the basic reasons why water exercise is so good for you – and why your water gym should be an important spot in your life. That 'lift' you get in water will be a great boon to you when it comes to the sense of wellbeing, recovery and prevention.

Avoid heat loss, though. When you have an arthritic condition, the exercising of any joint's bones, muscles and ligaments must be done under the best conditions. It's not going to be of much use at all to try to get exercising benefits if you're getting cold. This applies to dryland exercising, as well as water exercising, but is obviously more of a problem in water.

If you've an outdoor pool, only use it in warm weather and, even then, after warming up. At other times, take advantage of the heated, year-round pool facilities in your neighborhood – health clubs, or public amenities or clinics, and the like.

The increased flexibility that comes from water exercising permits greater ease and range of motion for ailing muscles. Improvement is not just from the exercise itself, but from the 'new' awareness you will get about how to move without pain against the gentle resistance of water. In water, it will seem much clearer to you which muscles or joints you are using, for that is in the nature of the higher perceptions about your environment that you get when immersed. You are able to focus the water itself, your exercise and your breathing on the area that is causing you pain or discomfort. This will tend to alleviate the problem more readily, if only because you learn and comprehend alternative ways of using your muscles to bypass the afflicted area.

Remember to start out slowly, avoiding any sudden movement or strain to your sore part. Even the superfit have to follow this basic.

The type of exercises you will do will depend on your individual condition. Whichever you choose, go for doing them for as long as you can – in other words, exercise for endurance. Strength enough will come from getting your exercising done over longer, continuous periods.

Choose from the suggested basic exercises given earlier in this Chapter, but add variety by consulting Chapters 9, 10, 11 and 12.

Adapt exercises to your special needs by using a little imagination without being too adventuresome. The following samples will demonstrate how you can very simply vary the basic exercises for your own special needs.

SPECIAL HALF PRESS-UP
Stretcher/Flexer
Standing
Benefits: hands and wrists

This is a variation on Exercise 17. Each time you take some or all of your weight against the wall, change the position of your fingers as you require. These can be: fingers spread apart; fingers bunched; one or two fingers outstretched while the other fingers are bunched; the hands forming raised bridges; and so forth. Hold each position for good stretch. Repeat as necessary before changing positions.
Likewise wrist positions. These can change, say, by: pointing fingers outwards; pointing fingers inwards; pointing fingers upwards; placing clenched fists flat against side; and so forth.
Note: Don't be too vigorous in your pressing-down movement. Instead, take your weight slowly. The water will assist you to determine how much of your weight to apply and for how long.

SPECIAL DANGLE ROUNDERS
Stretcher/Flexer
Sitting
Benefits: feet and ankles
especially, thighs, calves

This is a variation on Exercise 13. Instead of rotating ankles swing feet and ankles through a wider range of movements. These can be: turning soles out, turning soles in; cocking feet and spreading toes, then relax, then repeat; point feet downwards as far as possible and rotate as many times as possible in that position; with feet cocked, turning soles inwards and outwards in continuous motion; and so forth.

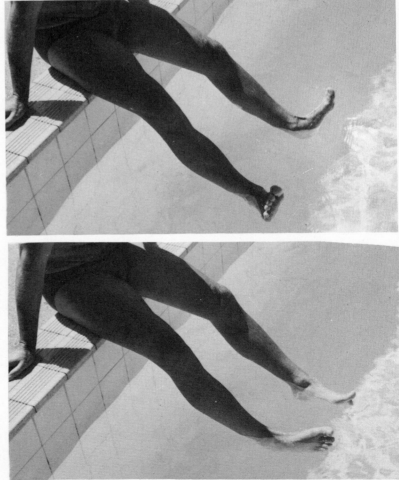

SPECIAL ARM ROUNDERS
Flexer
Standing
Benefits: wrist and hand especially; also arms and shoulders

This is a variation on Exercise 12. Shoulder depth and arms open wide. Instead of, or after, circling arms, reach across body with one arm and hold your other wrist. Rotate that wrist clockwise and counter-clockwise. Use your fingers as 'paddles' as best you can to get benefit of the resistance of the water. Repeat holding other wrist on other side of your body.

—15—
Natural Environments

One of the maxims I used earlier was that we all should heed: *Keep on the go. Don't let life find you not wriggling.*

I was talking about letting ourselves become lazy and soporific, of course, through the lack of energy of a body and mind that are no longer in tune with their natural environments. Fitness programs, providing they are not grossly incorrect exercise programs, are the essential means by which we keep our bodies in tune with our natural environment as much as possible. Mental alertness, too, is certainly enhanced by a healthily functioning body that is coping as best as possible with all the poisons of modern existence; yet that is not to say that the mind is in tune with its natural environment.

We need to experience the higher perceptions for that. There are many ways through which human beings achieve a higher perceptivity. We could call them 'highs' or flashes of revelation. They could come from a religious insight, a moment of calm bliss while (say) on top af a mountain, or even a sports 'high' when the adrenalin is really pumping. It depends on a person's outlook, perceptibility, habits.

For me, it is the experience of the sensation of water.

It is the same for most people. Water adds that extra dimension to the business of *wriggling* in life which is open to each of us. In water we can reach the occasional state in which we can truly say that our minds are in tune with some natural environment.

When you add exercising in that element of water, you have an activity that is not just good for the heart or lungs and so forth. You have an activity which places us *wholly* back into a natural fitfulness within the scheme of things . . . in tune with the *wriggliness* of the natural world, if you like.

Only the human mind tries to impose its own nature by straightening things out. In a sense, everything in nature *wriggles.* There are precious few straight lines or right angles in the living world outside of our minds – plants and animals are not stiff and symmetrical; the natural world is not an ordered shape that could be plotted on a graph. We have put ourselves out of touch with our environment.

Well, water is certainly *wriggly*, while being one of the base elements of our world and of our thinking. Being in water allows us to relive that experience of the wriggliness of life. We experience origins. We become more in tune with the real nature of our environment and our genesis.

I hope you will reap both the physical and the emotional rewards out of water exercising. Do it regularly for its benefits, and so that you can improvise in order to realise its infinite variety. Let water nurture you again, as it has since the beginning of your life. Let it heal your body, and let it heal your mind.

But, above all, do it enjoyably.

Index to Exercises

Exercise	Exercise no.	Page no.
Joy of Spring	1	34
Calf Stretch	2	34
Storch Stretch	3	35
Front Fanning	4	35
Fanning Beneath	5	36
Fanning Vertically	6	36
Fan and Heave	7	37
Beacon 1	8	37
Beacon 2	9	38
Rainbow	10	38
Rainbow Circle	11	39
Arm Rounders	12	39
Dangle Rounders	13	40
Dangle Kick	14	40
Buttock Roll	15	41
Side Roll	16	41
Half Press-Ups	17	42
Groin Flex 1	18	43
Groin Flex 2	19	43
Back Swallow 1	20	44
Water Splits	21	44
Shallow Boxing	22	45
Sideswiping 1	23	45
Ballet Stretch	24	46
Water Squats 1	25	46
Water Squats 2	26	47
Dog Paddling	27	47
Chest Puffing	28	48
Hurdling	29	48
Water Disco 1	30	49
Water Disco 2	31	50
Corkscrew	32	50
Kicking in Place 1	33	51
Kicking in Place 2	34	52
Scissors	35	52
Back Tuck	36	53
Back Scissors with Tuck	37	53
Jack Knife	38	54
Push and Pull	39	54
Reverse Scissors	40	55
One-Arm Paddle	41	55
Wall Shove	42	56

Push, Pull and Shove	43	56
Ship Roll	44	57
Running on Spot	45	57
Astride Jumping	46	58
Hopping Mad 1	47	58
Hopping on Spot	48	59
Hopping Mad 2	49	59
Porpoising 1	50	60
Squat Jumps	51	60
Feet First Sculling	52	61
Paddle Fanning	53	63
Canoeing	54	63
Dangle Kick 2	55	64
Back Swallow 2	56	64
Sideswiping 2	57	65
Sprint	58	65
Hangman's Kick 1	59	66
Hangman's Kick 2	60	66
Hangman's Kick 3	61	67
Dorsal Flip	62	67
Somersaulting	63	68
Submarine 1	64	68
Submarine 2	65	69
Floating Tuck 1	66	69
Floating Tuck 2	67	70
Bicycle	68	70
Reverse Scissors Lift	69	71
Suspended Arch	70	71
Pendulum	71	72
Running	72	73
Ballet Bar	73	73
Body Ball	74	74
Flotsam	75	74
Water Walking	76	75
Star Fish 1	77	75
Star Fish 2	78	76
Whirlwinding	79	76
Porpoising 2	80	77
One-Legged Dog Paddle	81	77
Press-Ups	82	78
Deep Press-Ups	83	78
Back Press-Ups	84	79
Swimming in Place	85	112
Fanning Twosome	86	112
Touch Toes	87	113
Piggybacks	88	113
Jack Knife	89	114
Kicking in Place	90	114
The Supplers	91	115
Lounge Kicking	92	115
Dragging	93	116
Dead Weight	94	116
Jackboot Assist	95	117
Thigh Stretch	96	117

Jitterbug 1	97	118
Jitterbug 2	98	118
Coalman Ultra-stretch	99	119
See-Saw 1	100	119
See-Saw 2	101	120
Locomotive	102	120
Jiving	103	121
Bouncing	104	122
Pyramid	105	122
Spine Stretch	106	130
Scissors	107	130
Half Jack Knife	108	131
Tuck	109	131
Hips Twist	110	132
Back Push	111	132
Side Kick	112	133
Arms Fanning	113	133
Water Ballet Squats	114	134
Splits	115	134
Kicking	116	135
Horizontal/Floating/Vertical	117	135
Special Half Press-Up	118	141
Special Dangle Rounders	119	142
Special Arm Rounders	120	143

General Index

Note: The numbers set in bold type indicate the pages on which the exercises are fully described.

Abdomen/abdominal muscles: 25, 104, 105, 130, 131, 132, 133, 134, 135
Aerobic exercises: 22, 23, 28
Aerobics: 28
Anaerobic exercises: 22, 23, 24
Ankles: 25, 94, 95, 96, 115, 117, 135, 138, 142
Arm Rounders (exercise): **39**, 81, 83, 85, 106
Arms: 25, 81, 82, 83, 84, 85, 86, 87, 116, 118, 119, 121, 122, 133, 143
Arms Fanning (exercise): **133**
Arthritis: 15, 20, 110, 136-143 *passim*
Astride Jumping (exercise): **58**, 92, 96, 97, 102
Back: 25, 88, 89, 90, 91, 92, 113, 114, 115, 117, 118, 119, 120, 122, 124, 130, 131, 132, 134
Back muscles: 25, 89, 90, 91, 130, 131, 132, 134
Back Push (exercise): **132**
Back Scissors with Tuck (exercise): **53**, 86, 89, 91, 95, 96, 102
Back Swallow 1 (exercise): **44**, 81, 87, 89, 110, 139
Back Swallow 2 (exercise): **64**, 86, 88, 90, 106, 110
Back Tuck (exercise): **53**, 85, 88, 89, 91, 95, 104
Ballet Bar (exercise): **73**, 94, 96, 99
Ballet Stretch (exercise): **46**, 89, 98, 107
Beacon 1 (exercise): **37**, 100, 101, 107, 109, 139
Beacon 2 (exercise): **38**, 81, 83, 100, 101, 107, 109
Beauty: 18, 21,

see also Body toning
Bicycle (exercise): **70**, 82, 84, 92, 94, 98, 99, 101, 103, 105
Blood pressure: 19
Body Ball (exercise): **74**, 88, 90, 92
Body building/toning: chapt II *passim*, 10, 18, 21, 31, 125, 126
Bouncing (exercise): 122
Breathing: 18, 23, 33, 62, 125, 127, 128, 129, 136, 140
Buoyancy: 8, 13, 17, 111, 124, 125, 140
Buttock Roll (exercise): **41**, 91, 94, 104
Buttocks: 91, 92, 116, 130, 131
Calf Stretch (exercise): **34**, 87, 89, 93, 139
Calves: 25, 93, 94, 115, 142
Canoeing (exercise): **63**, 82, 84, 86, 100, 102, 108, 109
Chest: 25, 104, 105, 106, 107, 108, 109, 122
Chest Puffing (exercise): **48**, 81, 89, 104, 106
Coaching: 16, 17, 22, 126
Coalman Ultrastretch (exercise): 119
Cold: 25, 30, 129, 140
Corkscrew (exercise): **50**, 89, 95, 102
Couples: 20, 111
Dangle Kick (exercise): **40**, 91, 93, 94, 100, 101, 139
Dangle Kick 2 (exercise): **64**, 95, 100, 102
Dangle Rounders (exercise): **40**, 93, 94, 97, 101, 104
Dead Weight (exercise): 116
Diet: 19, 24
Disco, water: 11

Doctor (medical advisor): 20, 123, 136
Dog Paddling (exercise): **47**, 81, 83, 85, 88, 89, 93, 94, 97, 98, 102, 107
Dorsal Flip (exercise): **67**, 86, 90, 103, 105, 110
Dragging (exercise): 116
Endurance: 13, 14, 26, 125, 136, 140
Energy: 14, 26
Exercising, general benefits: 11, 13, 14, 15, 28, 80, 87, 110, 123-128, 137, 138
Fan and Heave (exercise): **37**, 85, 106, 107
Fanning Beneath (exercise): **36**, 81, 83, 85, 89, 106
Fanning Twosome (exercise): 112
Fanning Vertically (exercise): **36**, 81, 83, 85, 106, 107, 139
Feet: 25, 94, 95, 96, 115, 117, 135, 138, 142
Feet First Sculling (exercise): **61**, 82, 84, 86, 104
Flexing exercises (or Flexers): 17, 20, 24, 26, 34, 35, 36, 37, 38, 39, 40, 41, 42, 43, 44, 45, 46, 47, 48, 49, 50, 51, 52, 53, 54, 55, 56, 57, 58, 59, 60, 61, 63, 64, 65, 66, 67, 68, 69, 70, 71, 72, 73, 74, 75, 76, 77, 78, 79, 112, 113, 114, 115, 116, 118, 119, 120, 121, 122, 123, 129, 130, 131, 132, 133, 134, 135, 141, 142, 143
Flexers: see Flexing exercises
Flippers: see Swim fins
Floating Tuck 1 (exercise): **69**, 82, 84, 92, 101, 103, 105
Floating Tuck 2 (exercise): **70**, 82, 84, 92, 101, 103, 105

Flotsam (exercise): **74**, 82, 84, 90, 92, 99, 106, 110

Front Fanning (exercise): **35**, 81, 83, 85, 106, 139

Groin: 25, 96, 115, 122, 133, 134

Groin Flex 1 (exercise): **43**, 96, 98, 101, 139

Groin Flex 2 (exercise): **43**, 91, 96, 98, 101, 107

Half Jack Knife (exercise): 131

Half Press-Ups (exercise): **42**, 81, 87, 139

Hamstring: 25, 98, 99, 113, 116, 117

Hand paddles: 31

Hands: 25, 87, 138, 141, 143

Hangman's Kick 1 (exercise): **66**, 82, 84, 86, 88, 96, 97, 103, 108, 109, 110

Hangman's Kick 2 (exercise): **66**, 82, 84, 86, 88, 96, 98, 103, 108, 109, 110

Hangman's Kick 3 (exercise): **67**, 82, 84, 86, 88, 98, 103, 108, 109

Heart rate: 17, 23

Hips: 25, 97, 98, 130, 131, 133, 135

Hips Twist (exercise): 132, 139

Holding-on exercises: 27, chpts 9, 10, 13 and 14 *passim*

Hopping Mad 1 (exercise): **58**, 92, 93, 95, 102

Hopping Mad 2 (exercise): **59**, 92, 93, 99, 100, 102

Hopping on Spot (exercise): **59**, 90, 95, 97, 102, 104

Hunger: 19

Hurdling (exercise): **48**, 91, 96, 97, 102

Inflammation: 140

Injuries, assistance with: 11, 15, 20, 110, 136-138 *passim*

Isometrics: 14

Isotonics: 14

Jack Knife (exercise): **54**, 86, 89, 91, 99, 104

Jack Knife – for couples (exercise): 114

Jackboot Assist (exercise): 117

Jitterbug 1 (exercise): 118

Jitterbug 2 (exercise): 118

Jiving (exercise): 121

Joint disorders: 11, 15, 20, 110, 136-143 *passim*

Joy of Spring (exercise): **34**, 101

Kick boards: 31

Kicking (exercise): 135

Kicking in Place – for couples (exercise): 114

Kicking in Place 1 (exercise): **51**, 85, 87, 88, 93, 95, 96, 97, 99, 100, 102, 104, 108, 139

Kicking in Place 2 (exercise): **52**, 81, 96, 97, 104

Knees: 25, 100, 101

Lateral muscles: see Side muscles

Legs: 25, 93, 94, 95, 96, 97, 98, 99, 100, 101, 102, 103, 113, 114, 119, 120, 121, 135

Locomotive (exercise): 120

Lounge kicking (exercise): 115

Lower arms: 25, 83, 84, 85

Lungs: 23, 25, 106, 107, 127

Medical advisor: see Doctor

Music: 10, 11, 28

Muscle toning: 11, 13, 19, 80, 124, 125

Neck: 25, 110, 114, 117, 118, 122

One-Arm Paddle (exercise): **55**, 82, 83, 86, 87, 104, 108

One-Legged Dog Paddle (exercise): **77**, 83, 84, 91, 94, 98, 99, 101, 103, 105, 107, 108, 110

Open-age competitions: 22

Paddle Fanning (exercise): **63**, 82, 84, 86, 90, 104, 106

Pelvic muscles: 123, 124, 126, 129

Pendulum (exercise): **72**, 82, 84, 86, 90, 94, 96, 98, 99, 103, 105, 106, 109, 110

Piggybacks (exercise): 113

Porpoising 1 (exercise): **60**, 86, 90, 93, 95, 97, 99, 100, 102, 104, 106, 108, 110

Porpoising 2 (exercise): **77**, 84, 88, 90, 94, 99, 103, 105, 107, 108, 110

Post-natal period: 124, 129

Pregnancy: 11, 15, 20, 123-128

Press-Ups (exercise): **78**, 83, 85, 87, 88, 91, 105, 107, 108
  Deep: **78**, 83, 85, 87, 88, 91, 105, 107, 108
  Back: **79**, 83, 85, 87, 88, 91, 105, 107, 108

Push and Pull (exercise): **54**, 81, 83, 88, 108, 110

Push, Pull and Shove (exercise): **56**, 82, 84, 86, 87, 89, 93, 95, 97, 99, 100, 104, 108

Pyramid (exercise): 122

Rainbow (exercise): **38**, 81, 83, 107, 109, 139

Rainbow Circle (exercise): **39**, 81, 83, 89, 107, 109, 110

Relaxation: 10, 18, 28, 62, 80, 127

Repetition: 26, 80

Resilience: 14, 26, 127

Resistance of water: 7, 13, 26, 124, 128, 136, 140

Reverse Scissors (exercise): **55**, 86, 91, 96, 104

Reverse Scissors Lift (exercise): **71**, 86, 90, 92, 95, 103, 105

Rhythm: 8, 15, 18, 28, 62, 125

Routine: 15, 16, 17, 18, 21, 24, 29, 30, 80, 126, 140, 145

Running (exercise): **73**, 90, 94, 95, 98, 99, 101, 103, 105, 106, 108, 109

Running on Spot (exercise): **57**, 92, 93, 95, 97, 99, 100, 102, 139

Scissors (exercise): **52**, 96, 102, 104, 108

Scissors – pregnancy (exercise): 130, 139

See-saw 1 (exercise): 119

See-saw 2 (exercise): 120

Shallow Boxing (exercise): **45**, 81, 85, 109, 139

Ship Roll (exercise): **57**, 86, 90, 92, 95, 109

Shoulders: 25, 81, 82, 83, 84, 85, 86, 87, 112, 113, 116, 118, 119, 120, 122, 143

Side Kick (exercise): 133

Side muscles: 25, 107, 108, 112, 116, 118, 119, 122, 130, 131, 132, 135

Side Roll (exercise): **41**, 81, 94, 107

Sideswiping 1 (exercise): 31, **45**, 89, 91, 94, 97, 98, 101, 139

Sideswiping 2 (exercise): **65**, 90, 92, 94, 95, 97, 99, 102

Slimming: 19

Special Arm Rounders (exercise): 143

Special Dangle Rounders (exercise): 142

Special Half Press-Up (exercise): 141

Special needs: 15, 20, 21

Spine: 25, 88, 119, 130

Spine Stretch (exercise): 130, 139

Splits (exercise): 134
Stomach: 25, 104, 105, 106, 107, 108, 109, 112, 113, 114, 115, 116, 117, 118, 119, 120, 122
Somersaulting (exercise): **68**, 88, 90, 105, 106
Sprint (exercise): **65**, 86, 87, 92, 94, 95, 97, 99, 100, 103
Squat Jumps (exercise): **60**, 86, 92, 93, 97, 102, 106
Star Fish 1 (exercise): **75**, 82, 84, 87, 90, 96, 103, 105, 108
Star Fish 2 (exercise): **76**, 83, 84, 87, 103, 105, 108
Strength: 11, 13, 14, 24, 26, 125, 136, 138, 140
Stress: 8, 18, 19, 80, 127
Stretching exercises (or Stretchers): 13, 17, 20, 24, 25, 33, 34, 35, 38, 40, 43, 44, 45, 46, 48, 50, 52, 64, 73, 74, 112, 113, 115, 116, 117, 118, 119, 120, 122, 123, 129, 130, 132, 134, 136, 137, 138, 141, 142
Stretchers: see Stretching exercises
Stork Stretch (exercise): **35**, 94, 101

Submarine 1 (exercise): **68**, 86, 94, 99, 101, 105, 108
Submarine 2 (exercise): **69**, 94, 95, 98, 99, 103, 105
Supplers (exercise): 115
Suspended Arch (exercise): **71**, 88, 90, 105, 106
Swim fins: 31, chpt 10 *passim*
Swim goggles: 32
Swimmer (only) exercises: 10, 29, 61, 62, 67, 68, 69, 70, 71, 72, 74, 75, 76, 77, 135
Swimming cap: 32
Swimming in Place (exercise): 112
Synchronised swimming: 11
Thigh Stretch (exercise): 117
Thighs: 25, 101, 102, 103, 113, 114, 115, 117, 130, 131, 132, 133, 134, 142
Thirst: 19
Touch Toes (exercise): 113
Tuck (exercise): 131
Twosomes: see Couples
Upper Arms: 25, 81, 82, 83, 133, 134
Vigour: 8, 14, 15, 17, 18, 26, 80, 123, 125, 126

Waist: 25, 109, 121, 132, 133
Wall Shove (exercise): **56**, 82, 84, 87, 89, 93, 95, 99, 100
Warm-up exercises (or Warm-ups): 17, 24, 25, 34, 49, 50, 57, 58, 63, 116, 118, 121, 123, 137, 138
Water Ballet Squats (exercise): 134
Water Disco 1 (exercise): **49**, 85, 89, 91, 93, 95, 97, 100, 102, 104, 107, 109, 139
Water Disco 2 (exercise): **50**, 81, 85, 89, 91, 93, 95, 97, 98, 100, 102, 104, 107, 109
Water Splits (exercise): **44**, 96, 100
Water Squats 1 (exercise): **46**, 91, 93, 97, 98, 100, 102
Water Squats 2 (exercise): **47**, 85, 91, 93, 97, 98, 100, 102
Water Walking (exercise): **75**, 82, 84, 90, 98, 99, 101, 103, 109
Weight loss: 19
Wet suit: 30
Whirlwinding (exercise): **76**, 83, 84, 87, 90, 94, 96, 98, 99, 101, 103, 105, 107, 108, 110
Wrists: 25, 87, 138, 141, 143